PINK SLIPPED

PINK SLIPPED

A Post-Layoff Survival Guide

Edie Milligan Driskill CFP, CLU

ALPHA

A member of Penguin Group (USA) Inc.

ALPHA BOOKS

Published by the Penguin Group

Penguin Group (USA) Inc., 375 Hudson Street, New York, New York 10014, USA

Penguin Group (Canada), 90 Eglinton Avenue East, Suite 700, Toronto, Ontario M4P 2Y3, Canada (a division of Pearson Penguin Canada Inc.)

Penguin Books Ltd., 80 Strand, London WC2R 0RL, England

Penguin Ireland, 25 St. Stephen's Green, Dublin 2, Ireland (a division of Penguin Books Ltd.)

Penguin Group (Australia), 250 Camberwell Road, Camberwell, Victoria 3124, Australia (a division of Pearson Australia Group Pty. Ltd.)

Penguin Books India Pvt. Ltd., 11 Community Centre, Panchsheel Park, New Delhi—110 017, India

Penguin Group (NZ), 67 Apollo Drive, Rosedale, North Shore, Auckland 1311, New Zealand (a division of Pearson New Zealand Ltd.)

Penguin Books (South Africa) (Pty.) Ltd., 24 Sturdee Avenue, Rosebank, Johannesburg 2196, South Africa

Penguin Books Ltd., Registered Offices: 80 Strand, London WC2R 0RL, England

Copyright © 2009 by Edie Milligan Driskill

International Standard Book Number: 978-1-59257-962-4
Library of Congress Catalog Card Number: 2009929226

11   10   09   8   7   6   5   4   3   2   1

Interpretation of the printing code: The rightmost number of the first series of numbers is the year of the book's printing; the rightmost number of the second series of numbers is the number of the book's printing. For example, a printing code of 09-1 shows that the first printing occurred in 2009.

Printed in the United States of America

This book is dedicated to all my clients whose struggles and experiences have resulted in the advice and strategies that I hope will bring help and encouragement to the suddenly unemployed people who read this book.

Contents

Foreword

The Grapes of Wrath is part of the American subconscious—the tragedy of the Joads being expelled from their farm in Oklahoma. A sequel that might have been written is how the Joad family and thousands of others wound up doing very well indeed in California.

A comparable, if less dramatic, event takes place in all parts of the country almost every day. A worker or officer of a business is separated unexpectedly. Whether the separation is a layoff or a discharge, the psychological and financial effects of being "pink slipped" can be severe.

I am reminded of a Scottish children's rhyme, "What can a poor monnie do, with such a contrary coo?" What can be done? This book, written by my daughter, addresses this question with the hope that it may help those who are being given the dreaded pink slip. This book gives them courage to survive the ordeal, to remember that the sun will rise tomorrow, and, with luck, to think of it as the best thing that ever happened to them. Or at least not as the catastrophe it may first have seemed to be.

Since the years of the Great Depression, the federal government has created a variety of fiscal programs designed to help level out the peaks and valleys of our cyclical economy. The lows are neither as low nor as long as they once were. We rarely find entire communities or population segments unemployed for extended periods of time. Ironically, this improvement may actually cause a suddenly unemployed individual to feel a greater sense of isolation, which leads to the thought that if it isn't happening to everyone, there must be something wrong with me.

In my capacity as chairman of the Unemployment Compensation Review Commission of Ohio, I have become aware of the serious effects of finding oneself "between assignments." Edie has made her career giving counsel to the persons who are skating on thin financial ice. It is an unwelcome river to cross, but many have managed the crossing, and so can you.

William W. Milligan,
Chairman, Unemployment Compensation Review
Commission of Ohio

Introduction

In Ohio in the 1970s, you had to be 16 years old before you could get a real job. Being tall for my age (heck, I was tall for anybody's age), I figured I could tell potential employers that I was 16 and it wouldn't really matter to them that I was still 15.

Another by-product of being tall was that I was forced to learn to sew by the age of 12 if I wanted to wear anything that fit me. I really wanted to work in a fabric store, so I began stopping in regularly at the two stores in the shopping center a few blocks from my home, to see if they were hiring. It didn't concern me how many times I would have to bother them before I got a job. I just knew that eventually I would be working in one of those stores.

One afternoon, the manager of the larger store saw me walk through the door. Before I had a chance to say hello, he gave me this defeated look and sighed, "Okay, you can have a job." After making sure that my 5 (in 15) looked an awful lot like a 6 on the application, I started to work the next weekend. With all the time I had spent in fabric stores, I already knew most of what they needed me to know. I was working at full speed very quickly. Because I was the only employee without a car or a boyfriend (another by-product of being tall), I was willing to work on Friday nights.

Shortly after I was hired, a larger company out of Texas acquired the firm, and they sent up a new manager. She systematically fired everyone except me because I was the only one who liked working on Friday nights. That made me valuable. Every Friday night I would show up for work and there would be a new co-worker for me to train. It was a slow night, which made it a good time to train new employees. I became the de facto training coordinator. A couple of months later the store was fully staffed, everyone was fully trained, and we were working very well together as a team, I thought.

I loved the job and the people and the $1.45 an hour that I usually spent entirely on fabric. Then one day, with no warning, the manager asked me into her office and explained that sales were down. She was overstaffed and needed to let somebody go. She thought it would be the most fair to let me go because I was the youngest.

Until I began writing this book, I had forgotten about that real-world lesson that I had been handed at a very early age. I remember being mad more than anything and very confused. Could she really do this? Who could I complain to? This was so unfair! I was the one who had been there the longest. I was the one who had trained all the new people who got to *keep* their jobs. I was the one who always straightened the remnant table without being asked. And I was the one who would work on Friday nights. She'll see when her remnant table gets messy; she'll wonder why she laid me off. When she has people complaining about working on Friday nights, she'll wish I were still there.

At that point I really was 16 and had experience, so I found another job easily. Even though this experience didn't scar me for life, it sure did sting for a while.

I always thought that the range of emotions that I experienced following that event were attributable to the fact that I was young. Now I know that I was wrong. It was my youth that actually enabled me to bounce back, move forward, get another job, and not worry about it. The older we get, the more difficulty we have dealing with layoffs. Just like deaths and other forms of serious loss, it's something that we never really get used to. We develop strategies for dealing with them, but that doesn't mean they hurt less.

When we lose something dear to us, we grieve. My job in the fabric store was dear to me. It represented a level of accomplishment and responsibility beyond what most "16"-year-olds were doing. It represented my first step toward independence, and it really was a lot of fun. For someone to take that away, in a split second, with a lame excuse, made no sense.

The incidence of layoff is increasing this year due to a normal downturn of the economy, pushed to depths not seen since the Great Depression of the 1930s. Entire industries are on the brink of collapse, accepting massive government bailouts. Other industries are restructuring their work forces to try to weather the economic storm. Early retirements, rolling unpaid days off, wage freezes, benefit cuts, and other strategies are helping companies hold on to valued employees until the economy rebounds.

Layoffs, or temporary gaps in employment, have always been a threat to workers in down economies. Some of the laid off workers would wait out the downturn, some would retrain for other work, and some would accept unskilled assignments. With the unemployment rate over 10 percent in many areas, the unskilled jobs are all taken. The wait seems very long and it is hard to know whether new skills will make a difference.

In the past, layoffs were difficult, but the strength of the U.S. economy gave people hope that their distress would be temporary. While they were laid off, government and private systems kicked in to help out. But with a recession this severe, all of those resources are also stressed. These layoffs send people out into new territory requiring new survival skills, not just new work skills. Their homes are not sellable for a value they expect, their accumulated retirement savings balances are down up to 40 percent, and the tuition for retraining is more expensive than ever before.

These are not the layoffs of old, where an employer would hope that the reliable workers he or she had to send home due to lack of work would be right back the day the business picked up. The pain for the employer used to be the possibility of losing valuable, trained employees due to a temporary downturn in his or her business. But that practice became all but obsolete in the last recession of 2001-2002. The terminations were called layoffs but the employees were never expected to return. Many laid-off employees learned that their jobs were being reestablished less than a year after they were "eliminated." (See, I told you somebody had to work on Friday night and straighten that remnant table.)

That recession set new expectations for employers as they entered this latest and deeper recession. Many had outsourced key services or used contract labor during the economic expansion that followed, which made it easier to reduce costs quickly. They used overtime shifts instead of increasing the number of employees that would need to be laid off in the next downturn. Many of these strategies are helping companies hold on to a skeleton workforce. But the recession still feels the same to all those workers who were on contracts or working at the suppliers.

With these new corporate strategies firmly established, it is likely that every worker will experience a layoff or two at some point during his or her working life. But listening to these statistics is like listening to the highway accident tolls each holiday weekend. Intellectually, you know it happens all the time, but emotionally, when it happens to you, you still feel blindsided.

How to Use This Book

The book is organized to give you uninterrupted reading or a step-by-step process using the summaries at the end of each chapter and the many helpful appendixes in the back.

The 15 chapters begin with a discussion of the psychological impact that your layoff has had on you. They move on to cover the various areas of financial decisions that you will encounter. They conclude with how both your emotional and financial situation will impact your job search.

Each appendix is referenced by number in the section that it accompanies. You may stop at each reference and fill out the worksheet, providing you more in-depth understanding of yourself and the concepts discussed. You may also read on through and come back to those worksheets later.

Each section within the chapters ends with a helpful hint titled, "My Best Advice." If you have less interest in the topic covered, you may browse the main points by reading these highlighted tips. At the end of each chapter is also a summary titled "What You Should Know by Now." You can check your understanding of that chapter's topic by reviewing that list. You may then fill in the "Next Steps" list, giving yourself a summary of the ideas that came to mind as you read that chapter. You can review these lists in weeks to come as you move through your period of unemployment.

Acknowledgments

My kids, Will and Lydia, are my most honest critics. Will, age 11: "Mom, have you thought about the frame of mind these people will be in when they read your book? Dump the stupid analogies, get to the point!" And Lydia, age 9: "I was with you, Mom, right up to the soap-opera part."

Other, not-so-honest, but equally valuable individuals took precious time to help me meet the infamously impossible deadline. Paula Carlson and Jac Perkins typed at breakneck speed with impeccable patience. Joe Roberts, Seth Stearns, Lisa Sahr, and Pat Milligan gave me encouragement and confidence to dig into areas that once seemed remote. My husband, Paul, held down the fort as I disappeared into the trenches.

On the financial planning side of the world, I am grateful to the experts who clarified details and checked my facts: Jill Gianola, Teri Alexander, Jamie Sutton, Rebecca Hilbert, and those bound and gagged agents of huge financial services firms who cannot be named, but know who they are.

On the human-resource front, so many professionals came forward, eager to share their insights: Celia Crossley; Carole Tomko; Wanda Hambrick; Richard Needles; Bill Hollett of Drake Beam Morin, Inc.; Linda Leslie of Lee Hecht Harrison, Inc.; and John Challenger of Challenger, Gray, and Christmas. I want to thank them all for being patient with me and giving me the benefit of their wisdom.

Thanks to my editors who wound me up and let me go: Mike Sanders, Joan Paterson, Christy Wagner, and Jan Zunkel at Alpha Books. Their trust and professionalism is unmatched.

To the best bureaucracy I know, the Ohio Department of Job and Family Services, Unemployment Division. What a team! Joe Duda, Bill Anderson, Denise Carque, Paula Staggs, and LeAnn Raymond made sure Chapter 5 was perfect.

And I can't forget the tallest bureaucrat I know, Bill Milligan, the person I am proud to blame for my height. Thanks, Dad, for your long career of public service and your true devotion to family. This book is for you.

1

What Will I Do?

The only news that spreads faster than news of a layoff is news of a potential layoff. Just like the telephone game we played as kids, each time the news is whispered to the next player, it gets altered a little. By the time it gets to you, mere suppositions seem to be firm plans. Thoughts passing through your mind range from, "I do a good job; they'll never last without me here!" to "What would I do without this job?"

While rumors travel at lightening speed through your company and you may have heard them for months, it is hard to know how to prepare. The most common reaction is to believe that you will be spared in "this round." Your denial protects you from adrenaline overload and enables you to continue to do your job. When it comes, however, the news of your layoff hits you harder than you ever imagined it would.

Something Else

There is only one answer to the question of what you will do now that you are laid off. Something else! Even if you find a job doing exactly the same thing, you will be doing it for another employer. You may continue to *be* the same thing: a salesperson, a nurse, a secretary, or an engineer. But you will be *doing* something else. No big deal, right?

If so, why is the prospect of changing jobs so nerve-wracking? Because change is one of the constants in our lives that most of us never get used to. As much as we reward our entertainment industry for bringing us tales of intrigue, suspense, and adventure, we much prefer our own lives to be filled with predictable monthly payments that entitle us to view those episodes from the changeless comfort of our own safe living rooms.

Separation is one of the worst forms of change. Psychologists tell us that from the earliest moments of our lives, fear of abandonment (the worst form of separation) is what drives our relationships, our self-definition, and our mental stability. Add to that the fact that a layoff separates you from your source of income, the flow of money that continues to fund those predictable payments that create stability and that minimize other changes in your life. It's no wonder that a layoff is such a hard change to accept.

The layoff represents a potential change to other layers of your life. Your mental health and physical health may be challenged. Your relationships may be strained. You may find yourself moving to another area to secure employment or reduce expenses. You will have an opportunity to use these changes to create a much better life for yourself. It may be some time, however, before that new reality becomes clear to you. The interruption in your income is potentially the most disruptive part of this transition. You may not have accumulated a nice emergency fund. Or if you have, you would rather not have to spend it all after the long time you took to build it up. At this point, you don't know how long you will be without your full income. This uncertainty will make it difficult to know when to sell assets or incur debt. Your decisions will be conditional, but the conditions will not be known.

Expenses will be different, too. Some by choice, and some by necessity. Formulating revised spending patterns will take skill at a time when your focus really needs to be elsewhere. Communicating new financial plans as well as your emotional and practical needs to family members will take patience and sensitivity.

Whether your separation was an expected departure or a surprise ambush, you already know how anxious you are. The known is pretty awful—you don't have a job right now. The unknown is exactly that: unknown. You are entitled to your share of the anxiety supply available in the world. It is totally free and is yours for the taking. Appendix 1.1 will help you identify your biggest fears as you begin this transition.

> A male calf is born to a healthy heifer. She has now earned the title of cow. Her son's birth enables her body to begin producing milk, but he is no longer necessary. He squeals as he is separated from his mother. She moans for days, yearning for the connection to the life that sprang from her body.
>
> The market has responded efficiently to this cast-off of the dairy-production process. He is readied for slaughter and packaged as veal, one of the most treasured menu items in country clubs around the world.

The good news is that you don't have to be slaughtered to be treasured by the job market. You have been cast off to enable your company to survive a recession, or to be sold, or to go out of business. It had very little to do with you. It was about their stockholders. You may want pity, as many have pitied the male calves and stopped eating veal. But calves will still be born as long as we drink their mother's milk. And workers will always be laid off as long as the stockholders (that's us!) demand good rates of return on our investments every quarter. It was just your turn. So ready yourself for market and go do something else.

MY BEST ADVICE

You are the same valuable worker today that you were the day before you were laid off. Do not change your self-definition because of this temporary break in your productivity.

Why Was I Doing That Job, Anyway?

Whenever anything bad happens to you, there are always people who stand ready to point out the good part, the silver lining, or the lesson you will gain from the experience. I bet you just want to punch them! I know this because I've been punched a bunch. I've been through enough layoff journeys, working with my financial counseling clients, to know that everything works out just fine 50 percent of the time and really great the other half of the time. There are a lot of sometimes painful, but always valuable, lessons learned along the way.

One of the best parts of the process is to think back to the first day on your job. No, let's go back farther, to the interview or even the application. What were you thinking? Why did you want this particular job? Or didn't you really, but it seemed like the best opportunity at the time? Close your eyes and really go back. What did you think it would be like? What was important to you? What needs would it meet in your life? Write these down in Appendix 1.2.

Then fast-forward to one year, five years, or more, on the job. Was it what you thought it would be? Were those needs really being met? If the job wasn't meeting your needs, you have total permission to feel relieved. You don't have to be anxious. You could even be euphoric, if the stars are lined up right. How wonderful! You got out of a job that you didn't like and you get to blame someone else!

MY BEST ADVICE

Think back through the expectations you had of your last job. Did the job meet them? Or did you convince yourself that it did, because it was too difficult to change?

What to Take with You

If the job was meeting your needs and you really are anxious, now is the time to take an inventory of all that was good. No job is totally perfect, but it's important to analyze the parts that were more perfect than others. You will have more control over your future jobs if you know specifically what it is you are trying to recreate.

Appendix 1.3 is a worksheet that can help jog your memory about aspects of the job that worked for you. Work through it after a long walk or a good CD that you haven't listened to in a while. Clear your thoughts and then focus on the goodness from your job that you want to take with you.

You have built relationships on the job, some good, some not so good. Make a commitment to find ways to encourage key relationships to continue. You won't be seeing these people on a daily basis, so it will have to be more deliberate on your part to keep friendships going. The not-so-good ones will go away by themselves. This is a nontaxable bonus.

A problem you will encounter is that scientists haven't really discovered how the layoff virus is spread, and people who haven't caught it yet will be suspicious of contact with you until the incubation period has passed. In addition to being afraid of losing their jobs because they have talked to you, they may also be afraid that you will ask them to borrow money. They are also feeling survivor's remorse. On top of all that, they are exhausted because they are doing your job now in addition to theirs, for no more money.

You will be taking your job skills with you. Even if your boss thought OJT (On the Job Training) stood for *Okay, Just Try,* you still learned *something.* Don't overlook very valuable skills such as knowing how to work with very difficult people, finding ways to pull resources out of the air, and figuring out how to get things done yesterday. If you worked in a difficult environment, as most workplaces are prior to a layoff, you have probably developed some unique strategies that will be prized by your next employer.

You have gained some insight and opinions into how to work in your field. Your employer made mistakes and you noticed them. You may not have noticed the decisions that led to positive outcomes as quickly. But they were there and you learned what worked, also.

You also learned something about compensation strategies. How were you paid? What types of noncash benefits were you offered? What products were you able to buy through your paycheck? What worked for you and what didn't? What games did you play with your employer, the government, or yourself? What would need to be different for you to stop playing those games?

You are a different person than you were when you started that job. You know more. You have more to offer your next employer. Now is a great time to look for exactly what you need to carry forward with you. Do not allow the negative feelings you have about the separation to overshadow the years of growing, learning, and developing you enjoyed as an employed worker. Even though you are not currently employed, you are very employable.

MY BEST ADVICE

When a long, positive relationship ends in one bitter moment, it is important to keep that final impression in perspective. Your employer's parting treatment of you will not change who you are, unless you allow it to. Put a positive spin on the experience when you talk to potential employers.

What to Leave Behind

Do you know anyone who hasn't moved in 30 years? What does their basement look like? Can you say "piles of *National Geographic* magazines"? How about the garage? Is the car even in it anymore? The closets, the laundry room, the spare bedroom, and any other space not visible to the public, are probably packed with stuff.

Do they use it? Could they find it if they needed it? Would it even work if they did find it? Why do we hold on to things that deep down we know we'll never get any value from? It's a common pattern in our culture and creates a lot of very interesting estate sales.

We do the same thing with our work lives. We accumulate things that won't ever help us again, both tangible and intangible. How many old software manuals do you own for computers that died years ago?

What you need to do is to have a mental garage sale. Put out all the trinkets and toys of your past work life that are of no value to you and get rid of them. Take the skill sets and attitudes that no one values anymore and let go of your attraction to them. Especially get rid of the angers and frustrations that permeated previous work environments. Those are worth less than nothing. They are debts that need to be retired.

Then look at the financial decision-making patterns you have accumulated. How much of your current panic and frustration about changing jobs is directly related to previous financial decisions? Did you spend every penny of every paycheck, believing that they would continue forever, uninterrupted? Did you choose highly risky investments that would perform the worst during a time when you are most likely to be laid off? Did you commit to higher-than-affordable minimum payments on mortgages and car loans, given your currently unpredictable income?

Planning for the downside is not our strength as an economy. Salespeople are taught to squeeze every penny out of you. An emergency savings account is not held in high esteem, and actually makes most people nervous. So we save in tax-deferred vehicles that hold us hostage with high penalties and sales fees when we have an emergency.

Which of these popular notions have you bought into? It's too late to change any of the decisions of your past, but not too early to make a commitment to make different decisions for the future. With the immediate problems you face, you will find yourself wanting to defer thinking about longer-term planning strategies. This is normal. But this is one of those times when I will risk a punch and tell you that if you can capture the frustration you are feeling right now about earlier decisions—and decide which ones to leave behind—your financial return from this layoff will double.

Now we have a problem. I have just asked you to begin making changes at a time when your biggest problem is that you have to make changes! Why would you want to layer more changes on top of an already difficult process? Because, there is a difference between a negative change initiated by someone else and a positive change you decide to create from within. In a way, they cancel each other out. You begin the process of gaining back a sense of control and connection from scratch.

And you have the time! So many things you know you should have learned or figured out were put off because of the pressures of your day. Most of them won't take long, but you didn't even have that much time. This week you do. Use it well and give yourself a mental boost as you start accomplishing things that will give you a return for the rest of your life.

Not only will you be doing something else to bring in your money, you will be doing something else to manage that money. You will never understand more clearly than you do at this moment what that something else should be. Some changes will be subtle, like adjusting your 401(k) investments. Others will be more proactive, such as increasing the amount of life insurance you carry as individual policies, and decreasing your family's dependence upon employer-sponsored coverage. Still others will represent total changes in philosophy, like saving for major purchases instead of using credit agreements.

Adrenaline is a great teacher. We remember the deepest valleys and the highest peaks of our experiences because of this chemical. It's like a magnifying glass. A layoff usually falls into the category of a deep valley. And your adrenaline is pumping full strength. Use that to your advantage. Focus on the things that you know will benefit you in the future. Be careful of knee-jerk reactions to your frustration, however.

A positive change might sound like, "I've never really thought much about my disability insurance, and now that I'm laid off, how would I support my family if I became disabled? Maybe I should carry a private plan in addition to an employer's benefit."

A knee-jerk reaction might sound like, "I've always hated those darn credit cards. A consolidation loan would be a good idea right now, even if the interest rate is a little high. I'll get to skip a month's payments."

Completing the mental checklists that I have recommended in this chapter will bring you to a good spot to be able to begin working through the complicated process ahead of you. Appendix 1.4 worksheets will help you do it on paper.

This information serves as a foundation for many more discoveries. We will explore in depth the attitudes and feelings you are experiencing regarding this change in your life. Understanding it from your ex-employer's point of view is also helpful. You may not care two cents about how and why your company laid you off, but you should. Thoughtful consideration of your layoff will not only help you through your current anger, it will give you a healthy perspective as you plan your future career path.

With that groundwork done, we can then plow through the literally hundreds of possible financial decisions that you may make. We won't forget the most important one: how to decide where your next paycheck will come from.

MY BEST ADVICE

You have the opportunity to throw out the counter-productive decision-making patterns of your past. Turn the short-term loss of your layoff into a long-term gain by identifying new strategies that will bring you life long returns.

What You Should Know by Now

1. That you will definitely be doing something else soon.

2. What your greatest fears are right now.

3. Why it was that you were doing your previous job and whether it met your needs.

4. What good things from that job you will take with you to the next one.

5. What behaviors and attitudes regarding work and finances you will be leaving behind as you move forward.

Next Steps

1. _____

2. _____

3. _____

4. _____

5. _____

2

How Could They?

Game playing is a normal part of any job loss. As a matter of fact, we play "what if" games all the time. The "how come" games can drive us crazy. We try to put all the pieces together like a puzzle, but there are always a few pieces missing. We know people are not telling us the straight story but we don't know why. We replay everything that happened in the recent past, looking for clues. We vilify every person who could have known or should have known and didn't tell us. We feel duped, humiliated, and disrespected. We trusted them and we believe that they violated that trust.

It's Not About Fairness

You may be tempted to spend a lot of energy right now collecting proof that what happened to you and others around you was not fair. Even without showing me your proof, I can tell you that you're absolutely right. It wasn't fair. It never could be and it never will be. If you had the kind of parents who spent a lot of energy making sure that you and your siblings got exactly the same presents at each holiday, then here's another thing you can blame them for. They blew it. They taught you to believe in the fairness fairy. You're still walking around today hanging on to that fantasy. Write down all the reasons that it wasn't fair in Appendix 2.1 so you can prove it to yourself and move on.

There may have been some managers in your company who wanted to be fair to you. But, as much as they wanted to, they didn't have the power. Even layoffs that follow some orderly system, such as seniority, to determine who is no longer on the payroll, are still not fair in somebody's definition. You might define fair as morally right, just, or honest, but what you're really looking for is equality. The fairest layoff I've heard of was one in which everyone drew straws and had an equal chance of being laid off. This only worked because all of the employees being considered for layoff had equal responsibilities and equal productivity.

Think back, again, to how your parents treated you. If they flipped a coin to solve a dispute between you and your brother, it was probably a lot easier to stomach than had they chosen sides. The screams of "not fair" were the loudest when the decision appeared arbitrary or, worse, based on some untruth.

If you are a parent yourself, you know how much you enjoy looking forward to breaking up those fights. There are lots of ways to do it but none of them seem exactly right. What you didn't know about your layoff is that there was a fight going on amongst all the siblings in your company, maybe for weeks or even months. It might even have been a growing battle for years. It could have just happened because two companies merged. Or it could have happened because the competition has taken away a chunk of your market.

But whatever the cause, it was a fight. A fight between the status quo, the way they've always done things, and the profit levels that the owners were demanding in order to leave their capital in the company. And somebody had to break it up. Think about your kids again for a minute. What's the fastest way to break up that fight? I know you've said it at least once in your tenure as a parent. "Go to your rooms!" After a couple of slammed doors, you're going to find an immediate relief to the chaos that preceded it. Was it fair? No, especially not to the child who didn't start the fight. Was it effective? Sure was! Fight's over.

Let's add another little twist to this story and say that your mother-in-law lives in the spare bedroom upstairs. Each time your children fight, she comes downstairs and gives you the what-for about how you can't control your children. It's a lovely scene of family bliss and tranquility, isn't it?

I may not have to add anything else. This all may be making perfect sense to you. Our families are where we learn our problem-solving and social skills. We take those skills into big families we call corporations and we use the same strategies. The cranky mother-in-law is played by the stockholders. They remove themselves from the day-to-day turmoil, close their door, and watch their soap operas. When the noise gets too loud and their peacefulness is threatened, they step out and complain. When they complain, the parent, played by the corporate executives, has to do something and do it quickly. The children, played by you-know-who, get the brunt of this quick but effective action.

So now that we've agreed that it's not about fairness, what is it really about? The same capital system that attracted money to the corporation that gave you a job is the same system that laid you off. When you appeared to be productive and profitable to have around, you stayed. When you no longer appeared to be productive and profitable, you left. This in no way means that you did anything wrong. You may have done exactly what you were told to do and that's what may have been wrong.

It's true that a company will bend over backward to keep highly productive employees even during a time of slow sales or diminishing returns. So all we know about you from your layoff is that you weren't the most productive and profitable person on their payroll. Even though you may have met or exceeded all performance standards and hit every mark they gave you, they may have been the wrong marks. Your supervisors and managers may not have known what was needed to make you into a profitable employee.

It's not about fairness; it's about business. Business is one of the most inexact sciences we have. It's a series of trials and errors that result in either a success or a failure. Business is based on so many different variables that we can only guess as to why one particular formula or another actually worked.

MY BEST ADVICE

Stop replaying the games of your childhood. Even if you "win," it gets you nowhere. Learn more about what makes business profitable, and position yourself to do more of that for your next employer. That will get you somewhere.

What's Left of the Social Contract?

I'm going to spare you the history of an economics lesson. My guess is that you're not really in the mood for it. I would like for you, however, to think about your own history and maybe your parents' history as they've shared it with you.

You may be aware of a pattern of employer/employee relationships that has been around since the years after World War II. With a couple of notable recessions, the second half of the twentieth century was a pretty consistently expanding economic time. Most companies and corporations grew and thrived and made profits for their stockholders. The ones that did not thrive succumbed to competitive forces or poor management. Their workers, however, were eagerly recruited by other employers who needed their experience.

We all know people who went to work the day they graduated from high school and didn't stop for 40 or 50 years, working for the same company their entire lives. They got regular pay increases. They got turkeys every Thanksgiving. When their families were sick, their company's benefits took care of them. All they had to do in return was to be loyal.

Where did that loyalty really come from? Maybe part of it was from friendship with their co-workers or a particular supervisor. Some of it may have been akin to the brand loyalty that one feels for a hometown team. Another part of it was certainly due to the paycheck that was supporting their family. And after a while, it was a sense that all of those longevity raises added up to more than what they were worth on the open job market. I also bet a good part of their loyalty was just plain inertia. It's a hassle to change, and there didn't seem to be any good reason to.

Was their loyalty ever tested by a job offer from a competitor across town with a 25 percent pay raise? Or, worse, did their employer test it by handing them a 25 percent pay cut? How loyal would you be if those conditions were offered to you? In a free market economy you will work for an employer as long as it makes economic sense for you to do so. They will require your services as long as it makes economic sense to do so. Sometimes, what is referred to as a social contract was merely a situation where …

- It made sense for companies to hold on to employees for long periods of time.
- It made sense for employees to remain with the same employer for long periods of time.

It worked for employer and employee.

Yesterday, 20 percent of the workforce in the United States was working for a different employer than they were only three months ago. Only one quarter of those people who changed employers did so because they were laid off. That means that three quarters of the workers moved through a decision of their own. And this is the highest layoff period that we have seen in 10 years! Workers are leaving their jobs voluntarily three times as often as employers are asking them to leave. That's the contract. You stay as long as you want; they keep you as long as they want. Appendix 2.2 helps you see your history of job changes. How many were your choice as opposed to your employers' choices?

The Outplacement Model

When an employee chooses to retire or to leave a company, he or she normally does not cause trouble. There may be a party, there could even be gifts and cards, and there's usually some time to make the transition and say good-bye. Their managers don't usually throw tantrums and stomp around upset that the employee has made this choice to leave his or her job. They begin immediately looking for ways to get their work done and to fill the position. They may secretly be happy that the person is leaving or they may be devastated that they've just trained them and have them working well and now they have to do it all over again. But, whatever they feel, they move on and the company keeps going.

However, reverse the roles and the reality is very different. When the company makes the decision that the relationship is over, oftentimes employees do show anger and do look for ways to cause trouble. You may have been angry enough in the last few days or weeks to actually think of something that might have been very difficult for your previous employer to deal with. It obviously does you no good and it probably wouldn't have hurt them much, but it's a way to deal with anger. If you are having trouble banishing these thoughts, Appendix 2.3 might help.

Some people are not as self-restrained as you are and they act out on their anger. Talk to any CEO and they will tell you the stories of those handfuls of people who, throughout their career, made life miserable for them in the aftermath of a firing or a layoff. They'll tell you about the false unemployment claims, and the lawsuits, and the stolen secrets, and the lost customers. They remember it all. They hate it.

The folks who caused all those problems never really gained anything from their efforts except maybe a misplaced sense of satisfaction. What they usually did was scar their own reputations with employers to come. On the other hand, as a group, they did have some impact on the way that business is conducted. The efforts that employers now make to minimize the trouble caused by disgruntled ex-employees are something that we all benefit from.

The outplacement industry exists today because companies are very eager to do the right thing when employees are asked to leave. Is their motivation selfish? Of course it is. In all the years you worked for them, did you ever see them do anything that wasn't purely motivated by self-interest? You didn't, because that's not what companies do. They may have a benevolent mission in their company's existence, but their prime motivation needs to be to maintain that existence.

Outplacement services are not offered to employees because the company owes that to anyone. Only the top executives receive a promise of these services as part of their fringe-benefit package. Even so, the assistance offered to employees to find new gainful employment in some other company is one of the most valuable benefits a company could offer. Helping you sharpen your skills to ready yourself for your new job search is a priceless way to begin a transition.

MY BEST ADVICE

Take advantage of every piece of the outplacement services you are being offered. Don't wait to get started. It will help you keep your focus positive as you process your natural frustration over your situation.

Those Left Behind to Do Your Job

Chances are you've been at the other end of this situation. A layoff in your company sent home workers and left you to do their job. Remember how you felt when that was going on? Were you afraid for your job? Were you mad that the people who were sent home received severance checks that were monies that your department needed in order for you to work effectively? Were you mad that you were doing one-and-a-half jobs now and did not make any more money? Did it seem unfair that your previous co-workers were, what looked like to you, relaxing and having some fun until they found their new job while you were working twice as hard?

Those left behind in your recent layoff, in a sense, got sent to their rooms, too. They're feeling a little punished for something that they didn't do and are having to put up with the ongoing stress of the underlying problems that led to the need for a layoff in the first place. They will be reexamining their own job security on a daily basis for weeks to come. They will be reassessing their own priorities while having to adjust to a new work environment.

The only thing different from your situation is that they still have their paychecks and they are not yet in job searches. Their security in their jobs is not any greater than yours was the day before you were laid off. The difference is that you know what happened to you and they don't yet know what will happen to them. They may have drawn the long straws during this round, but the short straws go back into the pile before they draw again.

You have relationships with these people and it's important for you to stay in touch. They won't call you. They won't know what to say. They may think you hate them. They may think they'll be laid off if they talk to you. So don't wait for the phone to ring. Call them and tell them you're okay and that you miss seeing them each day. Let them help you brainstorm about your job search. They may need the practice soon, too. Ask them what you did well about your job and how you should sell yourself to your next employer. And give them tips about how you made your job easier. They will need the help.

In short, don't burn bridges. These people may be your future customers, your suppliers, or your competitors. They may be a resource for you at a time when no one else would know an answer you need. They are very important to you. Make a list in Appendix 2.4 of those you need to keep in touch with.

Others who were laid off at the same time are even more important. They will be going through the same steps you are and can give you support and encouragement. They may become employed before you and give you an entrée into a workplace. As well, they will become your network of problem solvers that will enhance your value in the workplace.

MY BEST ADVICE

Relationships take time to build. Don't throw away solid business relationships when you need them the most.

What You Should Know by Now

1. The kind of games your brain is trying to get you to play.
2. How important fairness is to you and how you define it.
3. Which pieces of your childhood or family life you've seen played out in your workplace.
4. What expectations of loyalty you have for former colleagues, former employers, and yourself.
5. The variety of outplacement services offered to you and how to take advantage of them—immediately.
6. Whom you will attempt to keep in touch with who is still on the job.
7. Whom you will attempt to keep in touch with who was laid off at the same time as you.

Next Steps

1. _____
2. _____
3. _____
4. _____
5. _____
6. _____
7. _____

3

Perspective Matters

You have two equally important jobs in the next few days, weeks, and months: managing your financial well-being and managing your emotional well-being. The plain truth is that you won't be able to do one without doing the other. If you focus entirely on aspects of your financial well-being—such as finding a job, talking with your mortgage company, and working your budget—but ignore your emotional well-being, your situation may begin to crumble. If, on the other hand, you postpone all tangible and tactical decisions regarding your financial life until you have regained your emotional stability, you may wake up one day to find yourself totally sane but with nowhere to live.

These two tasks are no different than any two assignments you may have been given at work that needed to be completed in similar time frames. Think about how you liked to handle that sort of challenge. Did you block out certain portions of the day to work on each? Did you like flipping back and forth between them throughout your day? Did you like to get up in the morning and know that you were working on one specific task that day and the other one would wait until the next day? Look for a balance between these two projects. You'll find a way to integrate them that will be comfortable for you.

The only mistake you can make is to ignore one completely in favor of the other. If your mental health has been relatively good in the past, then you may not totally understand what I'm talking about yet. Your path to emotional well-being following your layoff will more than likely be fairly quick. However, you'll still have to go through the process.

Likewise, if you've been fairly solid financially, you will weather this layoff with a few easy decisions and be well on your way toward a secure financial future. But there will be *some* decisions that you need to make. If you ignore either of these areas—the financial or the emotional—you may see consequences down the road that could have been avoided. Everything from an extra tax bill to a divorce are situations encountered by people who believe that things will just take care of themselves.

The Grieving Process

Whether you know it yet or choose to admit it, you are grieving. Grief is a term used to describe the range of emotions that we feel when we experience a loss. These emotions can come in rapid-fire succession, like rounds from an automatic weapon, or they can come slowly over a long period, like an intermittant software problem that you can't quite put your finger on. You can cycle back through them. You can experience them simultaneously. Everybody does grief differently. And with each loss we experience, we may process our grief a little differently.

One of the things that people report when they experience a loss is a flashback to earlier losses. You need to look out for this occurrence. The way you were treated by your supervisor on the day you were laid off can remind you of the last interaction that you had with an ex-spouse. The separation you feel from co-workers or customers may feel like the separation you felt when you graduated from school.

Psychologists talk about grieving as a process that needs to be finished. If you've had earlier losses where you didn't finish that process, your brain has an interesting strategy of recalling them to be packaged with your current loss as you grieve. It's pretty efficient, if you think about it. If you're taking this loss harder than you would expect to be, the answer may be that you are not only processing this loss but other unfinished business from your past. That may mean that you have become skilled at putting your grief on the shelf and leaving it there to be dealt with later (whenever that is).

In this section, we'll talk about some of the simpler steps that have worked for others, to begin to process your grief. However, you should consider seeking professional counseling to learn how you can do it effectively. It's hard for me to recommend spending money on professional counseling at a time when your income has just dropped, but these services may continue to be available to you through your employee assistance program (EAP) or through your health insurance benefits for a short time. Take advantage of that benefit while it's available. Beyond that, community health services and community support groups may be available to you at little or no cost.

Denial has been given a pretty bad rap in our culture in the last few years. There is a presumption that denial is a bad thing. Denial has a true biological purpose to enable a human to continue functioning in the face of tremendous grief. If you felt every feeling that you had after a tremendous shock, you might just shut down under the weight of it all. Denial is like a guard at the door that only lets in the emotions that you are ready to deal with. The only problem with denial is that if you don't send the guard home at some point, allowing those emotions to come through, they keep banging at the door for years to come.

If they are still there when another loss occurs, you may not be strong enough to keep them out. So either on your own, with family members, or with the help of a support group or professional counselor, make sure to send the guard away at some point and begin the work of regaining your emotional well-being. The sooner the better. I have met with hundreds of individuals who have shared stories of financial decisions that they made during a period when they were in denial. In many cases, they were still trying to undo the difficulties that they caused themselves.

In Appendix 3.1, I've given you a list of feelings that you may be experiencing right now. This is a place to start to look for the impact that your feelings are having in your life right now. Look over the list and circle any feelings you are aware of. Throughout the early process of managing your emotional well-being, you may identify with words on the list that are holding you back from functioning in a way that you are used to. By merely acknowledging each feeling, you have taken the most important step toward working through the ones that are holding you back.

Get out the list two or three times a day until you are back to yourself. By comparing your answers to the last time you checked, you will see that you are constantly changing. Your brain is processing this change and finding your center. Eventually you will be able to answer the question, "What am I feeling?" without looking at the list. At some point, very soon, you will be back to a normal balance, for you. Some days will be great, some rotten, and most right in the middle.

Appendix 3.2 gives you a list of possibilities for the second thing you need to identify each day: your needs. No one can tell you what you are feeling and no one can tell you your needs. You will have to do this yourself. You can't begin to know how to fulfill your needs until you know what they are. Others around you will be totally clueless, as well. They will project their own needs onto you, believing that you must have the same issues that they do. That doesn't help you much and may cause conflict. You own the responsibility of communicating your needs. You should share each need that feels urgent, realistic, and respectful.

If you are not back to your old normal self in a few weeks, I recommend that you see your doctor. You may be ill, due to the stress of your layoff. Your brain may be having trouble finding a balance and be leading you into the disease of depression. If you have had this disease before, you will recognize it and know what treatment is effective for you. If you have not had it, your doctor will discuss various options and find a solution. It is so important that you not let any illness, physical or mental, go untreated. You can't afford not to be well right now.

Taking care of yourself is the only way you will be able to move on to your next career step. Your mental health begins with identifying your feelings and acknowledging your needs. If that isn't enough, then professionals are everywhere who can take you to the next step. Find them quickly. Appendix 3.3 will help you learn the common symptoms of depression and when to look for treatment.

MY BEST ADVICE

Grieve well. Do it in style. Honor yourself and be aware of the importance of what you've lost. Be proud of the fact that you took your job seriously and, because of that, it hurts to let it go.

Loss of Identity

The answers to the following two questions will tell us a lot:

1. Who were you the day before you lost your job?
2. Who are you today?

If the answers to those two questions are not exactly the same, then you've got some work to do. If you answered the first question with something like, "The purchasing manager at ABC Company" and the second with something like, "An unemployed person from Springfield," you've lost your identity.

If, however, the answer to the first question was, "A nurse and a mother of two," and the answer to the second question was, "A nurse and a mother of two," then your self-definition is still intact. One of the things that licenses do is to enable individuals to continue to hold on to their identity when they're not working. An accountant is still an accountant as long she has her CPA license, even if she is not currently employed or doing any business as an accountant. A loan officer, however, a function that requires no licensure, might not call himself a loan officer once he is no longer employed in that activity.

We all know that many licenses don't actually qualify a person to do what they end up doing. For instance, many attorneys are not actually practicing law, but they can still refer to themselves as attorneys as long as their bar dues are paid.

Let's take a hint from this distinction and work on rewriting the answers to those two questions. When I ask you, "Who were you the day before you lost your job?" put the answer in terms of what you were doing for your employer—not the status that your employer gave you. One strategy that employers use to encourage people to be productive and stay around is to find titles that will feed their egos and give them status within the organization. If you were handed one of those titles and you bought into it, you forgot that it was a rental contract. Believing that you actually owned it will cause you to have an overall harder time dealing with the loss of your employment.

Some settings within our society have taken this to the extreme. In the military, for instance, a rank or title is carried even when the job goes away. In that setting, being stripped of your rank is many times more devastating than being stripped of your position. Think about how much emphasis you placed on your rank or title in your previous position. If it was a great deal, you'll need to make sure that you include that in your grieving process.

As you wean yourself from its importance in your life, a new title should emerge that feels even more important. Give yourself the license to be who you really are. As you find the role that you will seek to play in your next productive activity, give it a name. Tell yourself that's who you are. If you were the purchasing manager at your last employer and what you really did was design purchasing strategies, then you might call yourself a Designer of Strategic Purchasing Plans. Now you know and I know that this new status that you've picked is not going to have a license anywhere. It may, however, have some sort of professional designation attributed to it by a trade association that you might seek to achieve. If it doesn't, then it's just your own self-defined profession. Today you are still that person and you own the title.

Just because you're seeking your next customer/employer, it does not mean that you have changed who you are. This is the very first step in designing an effective job-search program. Knowing who you are and what you are good at is essential to being able to convince your next customer that they should pay you to do it for them. Instead of thinking of yourself as an employee who waits to learn what your employer has in store for you next, you become the designer of your own economic activity.

This is a concept that makes sense as you see people go out into the business world as consultants. They define their role, their title, their job, and then locate customers who can use their services. Even if you are more comfortable seeking a specific relationship as an employee, this perspective on your role in the economy is very positive. It gives you a solid sense of self-esteem that will be projected onto prospective employers or customers.

Even if you choose to take a position outside your optimal field, you will still define yourself as who you are, but as working in a different capacity at the moment. A physical therapist who takes a job as a waitress does not become a waitress. She is a physical therapist, *working as a waitress*. When she secures her next career position, she is a physical therapist, *working as a physical therapist*. She can say this with little hesitation because she has a license on the wall that says she is a physical therapist. Give yourself a license to be who you are. Let it describe you to yourself and to others. Your identity is yours alone to control. An employer cannot give that to you nor take it away.

MY BEST ADVICE

Allowing anyone else to define your identity is dangerous. Pick a definition you like and run with it. Make sure your job title is an adjective modifying your identity, not a noun defining it.

Family Communications

One of the hardest things to do after a job loss is face your family and explain what's happened. As hard as it is, however, most people find out that it's one of the more reassuring and healing steps that they can take. Appendix 3.4 gives you an opportunity to list the different people in your family who you might want to talk with about what's happened. It's best to be honest and uncomplicated in your message. A simple conversation might begin as follows:

I'm no longer working for ABC Company as of (fill in the blank). I'm planning to continue my career as a (fill in the blank) by seeking a new employer who can use my services. I am feeling (fill in the blank) at this point and what I need from you is (fill in the blank). I think it's important that you also learn what your feelings are about this and what your needs are. I would like to talk with you about this on a regular basis as we move through this process.

Back in the first section of this chapter, you practiced identifying your feelings and identifying your needs. These are the people whom you share them with. If you don't fill in the blanks in the statement above, your family members will fill them in for you. They will project their own feelings onto you and they will project their own needs onto you.

You will find very quickly that it's you they love and not your job. They may not even have known much about what that was. They want you to be happy and secure and they want to know that they're taken care of, too. If they were dependent upon you in any way, they will need reassurance and ongoing honest status reports as to what's coming next.

Small children need to know that their relationship with you will stay about the same. They may even actually enjoy your period of unemployment because you'll have more time to spend with them. But, their needs are very simple and their flexibility is the highest. If you need to move or you need to change your schedule, they will adjust the quickest with the least amount of dissension. They are also the most intuitive. They sense immediately when you're sad or frustrated. They will internalize responsibility for your emotions unless you explain to them how it's not their fault. If you can give them some small task, like putting postage on resumes, to help them feel a part of your job search, they will feel empowered and happy to help.

School-age children will be a little more critical and will attempt negotiating to maintain their piece of the dwindling pie. Helping them to understand how conserving resources and holding up their part of the household chores would not be judged as child abuse. This helps them to take up an active role in the solution to the problem and teaches them a valuable life lesson. For instance, if they have to stop their piano lessons for a while, it doesn't mean that they can't keep practicing the skills they've already developed. If the family is doing without the regular Friday night pizza, they can help learn how to make pizza at home and be engaged in the process of solving problems with limited resources.

As a part of the problem-solving team, they will create less friction and be more resilient if big decisions, such as relocation to a new state, have to be made. They won't feel as much as though this is something terrible that you're doing to them, as much as it's a decision that the family has made together.

Remember that their feelings will be just as complicated and complex as yours. They may not be as willing to voluntarily share their frustrations and fears. It is your job as a parent to help them understand that those are very normal feelings and that it's okay to talk about them. They have the same, maybe even greater, powers of denial, and it's important not to let this current crisis fester for processing sometime in their adulthood. Let them work it through now with you, as a family, rather than hold onto it and have to deal with it as an adult the first time they lose a job. Both the emotional and financial lessons that can be learned in this experience will be invaluable to them as they approach their own adulthood as an emotionally and financially sound individual.

Spouses are another matter altogether. If your relationship with your spouse was complete and loving prior to the layoff, it will probably become even stronger during this challenge. If there were problems and stresses that hadn't been resolved prior to the layoff, this period of unemployment may be extremely difficult to deal with. Once again, it's hard to recommend counseling during a time when your income is lower, but I will suggest that the last thing that you want to pay for right now is a divorce, and it's very difficult to search for work when you're having marital problems.

There is very little to be gained from being secretive or by keeping ongoing progress away from family members. If you explain the results of interviews or application processes, they can be very clear as to what the energy is that you're spending and the activity that you're engaged in. Scheduling a regular meeting to update everyone at the same time on how it's going is probably the best solution. This way they won't bug you when you don't want to be bugged, and they'll know when they're going to get new information. If you're clear with them as to your current feelings and your current needs, then they can be part of the process and not deter you from your goal. If you're not clear, they can only guess and will possibly interrupt or aggravate the process. Extended family is another group in your life who will be eager to help, but won't quite know how close to get to the situation. You should have the same conversation that you had earlier in the chapter with those folks. The amount of the information or the extent of the needs may not be communicated the same, but they still need to hear that you're okay and that you're moving forward. They need to have a small piece of the picture so that they can help. If you want them to have nothing to do with it, then your needs would be communicated as, "I need you to know that I'm okay and that I don't need anything from you."

Just like the small children, you might find some little piece of it that they can take care of for you, which will let them feel involved and give them some sense that they have been there for you when you needed it. Something that they can do for you, which makes a tremendous amount of difference in many job searches, is to open up opportunities for you to apply or interview with companies that they know.

We'll talk later about family loans, but at this point it would be best to defer to a later date any conversations about financial challenges or assistance that extended family members might be able to offer. If they bring it up, your response can be that you haven't really sorted that all out yet, and you'll let them know how they can help when you do.

With your immediate family, however, this subject of the family's finances should be brought up immediately and continuously throughout your unemployment period. If you have a severance package or final payments that will continue your income for a period of time, then that can be communicated right up front. Send the message that you need to begin to prepare for a time when income might be lower. Gather ideas from the family as to how you might accomplish that. If the budget needs to be cut immediately, it's best not to come to the first conversation with an edict of what you've decided will be cut. If you ask for feedback first and reserve your edicts for later, you'll find that cooperation will be much greater.

Affirming the Challenge

Now that I've convinced you to be totally honest with your family, I need to teach you to lie to yourself. Self-improvement books talk at length about setting goals, affirming changes that you desire, visualizing your future, and being the master of your own destiny. What all of these concepts have in common gets down to a simple little technique: lying.

Now that I have your attention, let me explain. You're taught from a very early age that lying is wrong. Many times, the punishment for crimes is not as great as the punishment for lying about the crimes. We all watched Nixon get into more trouble for trying to cover up a wrongdoing than for the trouble he would have experienced for the initial crime. Lie detector tests are based on the premise that your body behaves differently on a physiological level when you're lying. Your heart pounds faster, your temperature rises, and your breathing speeds up. In a word, lying makes us uncomfortable. Hold on to that thought for just a minute.

Let's talk a little more about change. At the beginning of the book, we acknowledged that change is something we naturally avoid. We don't like it when others impose change on us when we're not ready. And change that is generated from within is normally in response to some feeling of being uncomfortable. If the room is too hot, we change the thermostat. It the car is running a little loud, we change the muffler. If our clothes are all sweaty after a workout, we shower and change them.

So far we've got this: Lying makes us uncomfortable, and being uncomfortable is a motivator to change. Next, we need to talk about how our brains work in a simple way. Over our lifetime we receive messages. We begin with messages from our parents and we add messages from many other people in our lives, our cultural institutions, and our media. Think of your brain as a very complicated computer, and all of these messages are like little programs that make it run.

But wait! Some of them are like viruses. They got into the hard drive of our brains without us even knowing it. Now, they're controlling the function of our brain from behind the scenes. Sometimes our brains don't respond logically to situations. We might step back and wonder, "Where did that come from?"

If your computer starts behaving illogically, you look for programs that might be performing incorrectly. And sometimes you might even find a virus. The solution is to rewrite or re-install those programs that were infected.

The messages from your previous employer, when they laid you off, will behave like a virus in your brain. It will take some deliberate reprogramming to override those messages that may cause irrational thoughts. This will be necessary in order for you to move forward and regain normal functioning.

So now we know the following:

1. Lying makes you uncomfortable.

2. Being uncomfortable leads to change.

3. Your brain relies on stored messages to determine its functioning.

4. You currently have a message acting like a computer virus running around in your brain.

Let me show you how to use all this to your advantage. The message from your employer when they sent you out the door was a very clean and simple message:

You're a person without a job.

But as your brain absorbed that message and its viral tendencies took over, it may have been converted into one of these messages:

You're a person who doesn't deserve a job.

You're a person not worthy of a job.

You're a person who will never have a job again.

Now try this. Reprogram those thoughts to, instead, be this:

I am a person with a job.

You will immediately interpret that message as a lie. You don't have a job. How can you tell yourself you're a person with a job? The interesting part about our brain computers is that if you program this in and get it in there deep enough, then you will begin behaving as though you have told a lie. The uncomfortable feeling that erupts from that will cause you to make sure that you're not lying and you will find a job.

I have watched people set financial goals and personal goals for many years. Their initial inclination is to state the goal as something that *will* happen in the future. This fails our test for effectiveness because it is not a lie. I can state or predict that anything will happen and no one can call me a liar. As soon as I state it in the present, it becomes a lie. Because, if it's already true, it's not a goal. It's just a statement of my current condition.

Another tendency that I've seen is for people to state goals in the negative. They will list things they don't want to do or be anymore. For instance, they won't be in debt or they won't be behind on their bills. Just like computers, our brains have to be told what to do, not what not to do. So instead of giving it an instruction to not be in debt, we might instead give the instruction to have sufficient emergency savings.

Another common tendency is for people to want to set goals for those around them more than for themselves. People around you may choose to change but it won't be for your reasons, it will be for their own reasons. You may be the catalyst for change, especially if you're the one making them uncomfortable, but their decisions to resolve that uncomfortable feeling will be their own. How they do it will be their own choice.

The best time to reprogram your most personal computer, your brain, is early in the morning and late in the evening when you're alone with your thoughts and your brain is more relaxed. Start by choosing a simple statement that speaks only about yourself, speaks in the positive, and speaks of the present. Fill in the blank:

> I enjoy the financial stability that working as a _____ affords me.

This fits all of our criteria. The subject is "I," the verb is in the present, and it's a very positive statement. But more than that, it's a bold-faced lie! You're not working, you're not enjoying a thing right now, and you feel as though you have no financial stability. Perfect! As you reprogram your brain to adapt this message, you will overwrite the current predominant message programmed in by your previous employer.

It's important that you don't share this lie with others around you. They will see it as a lie and might even feel compelled to argue with you. You need time to program it in without any interruptions. Estimates are that it takes about three weeks of concentrating on a single message to actually program it in. Imagine if it took that long to make one change in your computer. You'd go crazy. We're a little more impatient than that when we become uncomfortable.

When I first learned of these theories about 20 years ago, my initial reaction was one of fear. If this really works, then I have no one else but myself to blame for changes that don't happen for me. And the next set of thoughts that came over me told me that I really needed to decide what I wanted to happen next and go do it. For a kid just out of college whose whole life had been mostly programmed for her, that was a pretty scary notion. You may be in a position right now where things have been mostly programmed for you for quite some time, and this is the first time that you've had the freedom and the opportunity to make choices all for yourself. You will have a lot of well-wishers imposing their ideas of what your life should look like next, but it's really your choice. With that comes responsibility to make that choice.

MY BEST ADVICE

Choose a really good lie. Make it yours, make it positive, and make it now. Repeat it to yourself each morning and evening as you prepare for and reflect on your day. Watch what happens!

What You Should Know by Now

1. How you are going to schedule the work of managing your financial well-being and your emotional well-being.

2. That you are grieving and whether or not you are finishing your grieving for earlier losses as well.

3. How long you will allow yourself to remain in denial.

4. A system for identifying your feelings and your needs on a regular basis.

5. How you will be defining your identity from now on.

6. Which family members you need to inform and how you will tell them.

7. How will you engage your family members in your job search process to help them feel involved?

8. What lie you will tell yourself each morning and evening as you erase the viral messages installed by your previous employer.

Next Steps

1. _____

2. _____

3. _____

4. _____

5. _____

6. _____

7. _____

8. _____

4

Severance Confusion

Sometimes the most important decisions of our lives have to be made under the greatest pressure. Our adrenaline pumps and we get through them, operating on what feels like autopilot. Instincts take over and we usually survive.

I can think back to the time when my sister and I were shot at in an armed robbery in broad daylight. Then there was the time when I walked into the middle of a bank robbery with my two pre-schoolers. I bet you're thinking that smart people don't hang with me much anymore. It just isn't safe. You're right, but that's not the point.

I know that I was totally aware and focused at the time of each crisis. I know that I acted to protect my sister and my children. I know that dozens of loving strangers were there to help. I know that everything turned out just fine and that the bad guys went to jail for a long time. But, I can't tell you the details, like how long each episode lasted. That information is stored somewhere else. Others have filled in the blanks for me.

Shock does that to us. In the middle of a crisis, we are sure that we will remember every detail. And we don't. It's why the police have such a hard time getting eyewitnesses to tell them consistent stories. Our memories are barely reliable on calm days, let alone on a day that we suffer a crisis.

Unteachable Moments

So what does your employer do? Sends you into shock, puts a bunch of paper in front of you, and asks you if you have any questions! It works for them. What questions could you *possibly* have?

> Excuse me, Mr. Bank Robber, sir? Could you tell me how your deprived childhood led you into a life of crime? And I was just wondering, is that a real gun?

Later, we have lots of questions. A couple weeks after the robbery, I saw the guy on TV at a court hearing. I was really interested. I actually thought about trying to visit him in jail.

You will remember forever some of what you were told in the day or two after your layoff. Some went in one ear and out the other. Some you will think you remember but it won't be accurate.

The initial information is given to you in a definitive tone. It's final. There will be no debate. Questions would only delay the meeting, which you were hoping would end soon. So you didn't ask enough questions to learn what you really needed to know.

It's hard to reconcile, at that moment, how you are being treated. They trusted you yesterday, but not today. You are flabbergasted, especially if you are immediately guarded or escorted through the building. These people know you. They are your friends. What is going on?

Even if you had some time to exit, relationships will immediately be strained. You don't know what to say and they don't either. Your life is instantly different. How would you hope to know what to ask in this situation?

The better managers and human resource professionals will coach you through the issues that should concern you. They'll know what you will be calling to ask about in a couple of days and they'll try to give you that information immediately. But, that's no guarantee you'll remember it.

The best way to address your unpredictable memory is to write everything down. Keep a notebook and pen with you at all times. If you can, carry a small tape recorder with you as well. Make people repeat themselves. Make them wait while you write. Get their phone number so you can call them later for clarification. Date each note you take. Then read back over your notes each day and you won't forget an important detail. Make a To-Do list from your notes and check items off as you go.

If you have a spouse or partner, it's not out of line to ask if he or she can be present at important meetings and orientations. He or she will have as much interest in the information and be able to lend a second opinion to many important decisions in the near future. Since partners are one step removed, they will likely have less intense emotional reactions, and will be able to bring more rational thought to the situation during the early days of the transition.

The outplacement consultants will have convinced your employer to begin your outplacement services immediately for several reasons:

- It's something to do when you don't have a job to go to.
- It helps you redirect your focus to finding your next job.
- It's a good way to start processing your anger.

Your employer doesn't want you to sit at home and stew about this. That's dangerous for you and for them. But they know, more than anyone, how emotional that first week can be. If the outplacement package your employer purchased for you has a time-limited service available to you, you will need to maximize the benefit from that service in a couple of ways. Put your grief on hold as much as you can for the few hours you are in their sessions. You can get back to that later. And then reread all the information they give you on a regular basis until you are re-employed. It's not rocket science, but it will accelerate your search. Absorb as many of their tips as you can.

MY BEST ADVICE

Don't expect to remember everything. Record or take notes at important meetings. Ask questions as many times as it takes for you to understand.

Human Resource Department Perspective

People who do human resource work are there for one reason. They like people. Imagine a person who can't stand people actually choosing that field. They may end up there by accident, but they won't last long.

People who have chosen the field don't normally list *letting people go* as their greatest joy in their job. In fact, it makes most of them terribly ill. There are those who have become good at it, but they still don't like it. It's a very bad part of their work. It has been compared to the conflict felt by doctors who join the profession to save lives, but then have to be the ones to communicate the terminal diagnoses.

Though human resource professionals are motivated to go into the field because they want to work with and help people, they find out extremely quickly that their first priority is to protect the company. They are not your personal counselor, your agent, or your friend. They are there to enhance the company's ability to make a profit from your productivity. They will come to the discharge meeting appearing to be cold and uncaring. This is their role to play. They will try to keep the meeting businesslike and hope that no one cries, especially them.

Even with that mission, they are still human and they do understand your trauma over losing your job. They very much want to see you land on your feet and benefit from your transition. They can be a lot of help to you during this time if you let them. It actually makes their job easier when they can continue to help you after the difficult role they played in your discharge.

MY BEST ADVICE

Your human resource professional or manager did not enjoy giving you your layoff notice any more than you enjoyed receiving it. He or she just had more time to prepare. HR professionals are one of your most valuable resources. Let them help you.

All That Paperwork

Your human resource department (HR), with the help of your manager and the outplacement consultants, will have a packet of paper ready for you. Compared to the amount of stuff that you had to sift through when you were hired, it won't look like much.

HR will have summarized your dismissal and your severance offer in a single letter that will be very brief and factual. It won't go into a lot of detail. They will also give you information on the outplacement services they have purchased for you and your instructions on how to access them. They will probably ask you to sign something that acknowledges receipt of this information. If you refuse to sign right away, that will be indicated on the form, but probably won't mean much to anyone later. If you are the type of person who does not sign anything until you read and understand it, those practices will serve you well as you move through this process.

There are conflicting opinions as to whether attorneys are helpful at this point. Let's divide their services into three categories: interpretation, negotiation, and legal representation. The probability is high that your employer hired a team of attorneys who are skilled at labor law to draft your letter and the documents attached. The chances of your attorney finding something substantially wrong with the form or content of these documents are rather slim. With that in mind, you may still find tremendous comfort in having an attorney read them over and tell you that you are being treated as the law requires. This is not the most important thing for you to be focusing on but, if it helps you to delegate this task, then do it. It will be money well spent.

On points of negotiation the jury is also out. If you are involved in a large layoff where dozens or hundreds of your co-workers just received the same offer, it is unlikely that your company will want to spend any time negotiating a better deal with you. But a good attorney might be able to help you spot areas where the offer is soft and a company might bend. I'm not sure that they would routinely find enough gain for you to justify their fees, so this is a risk I would take only if I felt the need to use their services for the first reason. This doesn't mean that you should not ask for things that are important to you. It only means that it might not be cost effective to seek an attorney's involvement in the issue.

With regard to the issue of legal representation: What you need is a job, not a lawsuit. I know that there are people who have legal grounds to sue for their job back and recover lost wages, but you are probably not one of them. The odds are really with the house on this one. If you seek legal advice for one of the first two reasons (interpretation and negotiation) and your attorney believes that you have a good case, you will have a big decision to make. You cannot imagine how much time and effort even the simplest of lawsuits can take. This is time and effort that may be better spent designing your new life without this employer. Even if your attorney offers to represent you on contingency, which is a commission-based pay structure, where you pay only out of pocket expenses until you win, it will still cost you in the form of energy and focus.

Back to that pile of paper. The first thing to do with it is to make a copy of it for permanent reference. Some of the pages you will need to fill out and turn back in to someone. Make a copy of it after you have completed it, also. But keep blanks in case you want to change your mind and fill it in differently.

Then, of course, you need to read it. If you hired an attorney to read it for you, you will want to follow his or her instructions as to which items need your attention, signature, and so on. As you read it, make notes to yourself in the margins about questions that you have. Underline things you want to discuss. Don't get too wrapped up in the legalese. Once your employer made the decision to end your employment, their only goal was to help you and in doing so, to help themselves. They have no reason to try to trick or threaten you.

Then call your manager or human resource department and schedule a meeting to go over it. Try to have the meeting in person so you can be confident of the information you receive. Give the person a summary of the items you will want to discuss so they can prepare resources that might help you.

The documents you receive will answer most of your questions, but probably not all. There are always things the attorneys advise them not to put in writing that are important to you.

This meeting will be an opportunity to begin your new relationship with your ex-employer. They will be happy to answer your questions. You will have a legitimate reason to return to your workplace and see people you need to connect with.

First you will want to ask everything having to do with your separation from the company. They will know the answers or can find out for you. Use Appendix 4.1 to list questions you have as you think of them. Some things that might be important to you regarding your compensation are the following:

- What are all the terms of my severance package?

- How much will I be paid?

- On what schedule will it be paid? Will it continue to be direct deposited? Will I be mailed my check and/or stub?

- Will it be reported to the unemployment office as being paid out this week or over time?

- Which of my deductions will continue from my pay during my severance period?

- Which of my benefits will continue with the same cost sharing during my severance period?

- Which of my benefits will continue, but at my cost during and/or beyond my severance period?

With each benefit that will continue, you will want to make sure you have the proper forms to turn in to indicate your option to continue. You may have some questions regarding your relationship with the company and your job search:

- Can you keep your laptop or PDA for a while to help you with job-search efforts?

- Can your HR department help you research compensation numbers in your area or help you network?

- Can you have a reference letter from them?

- What will be told to your potential future employers when they call to check your references?

- If your company has merged, how will your length of employment be calculated?

- Can you apply for other positions in the company? Will your severance be affected if you accept a position?

MY BEST ADVICE

Spend your time reviewing the information you received. Stay very organized and keep copies of everything you need to turn in.

Immediate Decisions

The day before you were laid off you made dozens of decisions. The day after your layoff you will start making a new set of decisions that will also require you to use good decision-making skills. If you are over 40, you have 21 days to make any decisions by Federal law.

As you go through the paperwork and meet with your HR department, you should ask what deadlines there are for each form and decision you need to process. Write it directly on the form. Then make a list by date of the decisions ahead of you on Appendix 4.2.

I'm not suggesting that you wait until the last day to make each decision. I do, however, believe that it is very helpful to understand that you have some time to think and relax. Then, having a schedule will enable you to rank each item in order of its importance. For the first 72 hours you should only do three things:

1. Tell your immediate family.

2. Go to your outplacement meetings and follow their instructions.

3. File an unemployment claim, if your severance compensation is less than six months of your income. (The next chapter will cover this in detail.)

Any other decisions or actions you take during this time may be regretted later. You will need some time to process your initial shock and anger before you start changing your financial situation or applying for jobs. This is a time for you to start putting your situation into perspective and designing your next career step. It is not a time for making rash decisions or taking drastic steps. Slow down and take a break. Recharge for the effort ahead of you.

Look for ways to minimize the stress that your body is feeling right now. Light physical activities, such as walks, will do wonders to help your body stay healthy. Meditation or prayer can reduce the physiological impact of a crisis. Processing stress sometimes requires blowing off steam, however. Whatever works for you is fine. Some people enjoy screaming (in places where no one will call the police) or punching pillows. And don't forget to drink enough water and get enough calories.

It's also a fine idea to take some time in this initial period to count your blessings. You have many and they will become clearer to you each day. Eventually, this crisis will take its natural place in the summation of your life, somewhere in between broken bones and lost loved ones. And for many, it doesn't even make that list because it opens doors and frees up energy for new opportunities that weren't even imagined before.

MY BEST ADVICE

Spread out the important decisions you need to make over several weeks. Don't think you have to do everything right away.

What You Should Know by Now

1. That you won't remember everything.

2. That you need to take notes, write down everything that's important, and keep copies of everything.

3. When you will be meeting with your human resources representative to ask your remaining questions.

4. What questions you have regarding the forms you need to turn in and the decisions you need to make.

5. What the deadlines are on each decision.

6. What actions you need to take immediately and which can be postponed until you are more relaxed.

7. How to pace your important decisions to give each of them the time they need.

8. What specific steps you will take to minimize the stress your body is absorbing.

Next Steps

1. _____

2. _____

3. _____

4. _____

5. _____

6. _____

7. _____

8. _____

5

Unemployment Compensation

Here's a simple question: If you look out the window of your kitchen during a thunderstorm and a tree has just fallen on your car, who is the first person you would call? That's right! Your insurance agent. And why do you call your insurance agent? Because you have been paying premiums on your car insurance policy and you fully expect that your insurance company is going to pay to fix your car. They might even pay for a free rental car to get you around tomorrow. Can you think of any reason to wait a day or two to call? I can't. Does it seem reasonable that you would just go ahead and pay for the damage yourself? It doesn't to me.

Unemployment benefits are exactly the same. Your employer has been paying the premium. You are covered. You've suffered a loss covered by the policy. Make the call! You didn't blink twice each time you wanted a bill paid by your health or homeowner's insurance. You felt no shame in filing those claims.

There is a lingering misconception that the unemployment insurance program in the United States is somehow part of the welfare system. It is not based on need, any more than your car insurance is based on need. Your agent doesn't ask you how much you have in your savings account and offer to fix the muffler, too; nor do they deny a claim based on your ability to fix the car yourself.

Who's Covered

First, you had to be employed, as opposed to self-employed. If your employer gave you a W-2, you were an employee. If you got a 1099 instead, you were not an employee. Receiving a 1099 does not automatically rule you out as a covered employee, but you may have a harder time qualifying.

Second, you have to have worked more than a few weeks. If you have worked more than six months, pretty consistently, you are probably okay. Less than that and it gets complicated. Each state has its own guidelines, which are listed in Appendix 5.1.

Third, you have to be unemployed due to a lack of work. Another way to think about this is that you were released from your duties due to *no fault of your own*. If your employer fired you for a good reason or if you quit without one, you do not qualify for benefits. If you feel your employer's reason was not good enough or you feel you did have a good reason to quit, then go ahead and file. You should prepare to defend your case because your employer will likely challenge the claim.

Last, you have to be …

1. Able to work full time.

2. Available for full-time work immediately.

3. Seeking full-time employment.

You will be required to keep records of your job-seeking activity. This will prove that you are actually able, available, and seeking. Due to the volume of paperwork, the states monitor this on an audit cycle. It is an honor system, like income taxes. If you are picked for an audit, you must produce the documents. And just like dealing with the IRS, it doesn't do you much good to lie. If you tell them you submitted an application at XYZ Company, they will visit XYZ Company and ask to see your application.

If you were working for a temporary agency or an employee leasing company, you must give them a call and allow them the opportunity to place you in another assignment before you file. If you have decided that you would like to see the world before you return to work, you will be eligible when you return. You can still file now, however.

Turning down suitable employment can disqualify you from receiving benefits. That's a hint that you are not really able, available, or seeking work. The definition of the word *suitable* has certainly been debated heavily. Some of the conditions that are considered include …

1. What you did in the past.
2. Your prior training and education.
3. How much opportunity you have had to find a position in your field.
4. The distance you would need to travel to work and the transportation modes available to you.
5. The hours and conditions of the offered employment.

So you can be picky, just not too picky. You will not be expected to accept a job out of your field at half your previous income, working only on weekends. But you might be expected to accept a position working in your field for your previous employer's fiercest competitor on a schedule that causes you to have to change childcare providers.

Just as your layoff was not about you, you'll be happy to learn that unemployment insurance is not about you, either. It's really about keeping the economy going by pumping dollars into an area where an employer has failed to continue paying their workers. To prevent one company's problems from affecting other companies and beginning a downward spiral, the government designed this program to keep money flowing through that local economy as the displaced workers locate new employment. This huge insurance policy is a program of the federal government, enacted as part of the Social Security Act of 1935. They take all the money from your state and issue an IOU, which promises they will pay it out in claims, if needed. Then they hire the states to administer the individual policies and process the claims. So you are the insured; your employer is the premium payer; your state is the premium collector and the claims processor; and the federal government is the insurance company.

Because it is a federal program, you are covered wherever you live in the country. You don't have to stay in the area where you worked to be covered. Moving closer to where the jobs are is good for you and good for the economy. The rules of the state where you were employed will be used to process your claim.

MY BEST ADVICE

File your claim for your unemployment as soon as you know you are unemployed. If you are unsure as to whether or not you are covered, let your state figure it out for you. That's their job.

The Application Process

It really doesn't get a lot simpler than this. In most states you can …

1. Pick up the phone.

2. Dial the number next to your state in Appendix 5.2.

3. Say, "I want to file a claim."

4. Have the following items ready when they ask:

Legal name and Social Security number

Legal names, ages, and Social Security numbers of any dependents

Legal name, address, and tax identification number of your last employer (This information is on your W-2 or is available from your Human Resource Department.)

Your hire date and average weekly wage (Just guess—they'll have the real data once they find you in their system.)

Most states are also offering claim service online. More are being added all the time. Appendix 5.3 has a listing of the websites to check.

All states now have One-Stop Centers, established by the Workforce Investment Act of 1998 (WIA), which combine several agencies under one roof. These pleasant offices save you a lot of time and running around. You can file your unemployment claim and receive free services at One-Stop Centers, over the telephone, or on the Internet. Anyone can get core services such as job-search and job-placement assistance, including career counseling and a basic assessment of one's skills and needs, as well as some follow-up services. You can locate the nearest center to you on the web at www.servicelocator.org or by calling the American Workforce Network Toll-Free Hotline at 1-877-US2-JOBS.

Probably the best part of the unemployment insurance system is that it has gotten very fast at processing these initial claims. If you are used to a biweekly paycheck, chances are you will only miss one payday, but you must file right away. The customer service guidelines adopted by the states and monitored by the U.S.

Department of Labor are helping to get that money out quickly. Some states now offer direct deposit to speed up the process even more. Make sure you ask if your state has this option.

There are some common problems that can delay the processing of your initial claim. Most of these are common sense, given what we know about computers and large government agencies. If you have incomplete information it will slow things down. For instance, let's say your last employer did business as The Widget Shop, but was incorporated as Bob's Widgets, Inc. If you report your employer as The Widget Shop, it will cause your application to have to travel through a couple of different piles on somebody's desk before they figure it out. If you fail to put your Social Security number on an important piece of communication, they will have to stop and figure out who you are. Another pile.

Keep copies of absolutely everything. Record all phone conversations and in-person interviews. Who did you talk to? What did they need from you? What did you report? All of it. If, heaven forbid, they make a mistake, you will need to reconstruct your application. You can try complaining, but you will still need to recreate what happened.

MY BEST ADVICE

Have a special binder to store each and every communication back and forth with the unemployment office. Write down everything that they ask for. Copy everything that you send them. Include a log of resumés and applications you have submitted to prospective employers.

Benefits and Taxation

Once again, all the states are marching to their own drummer. Appendix 5.4 helps you begin to understand how your weekly benefit will be calculated. Each state also has its own minimum and maximum benefit listed in Appendix 5.4. This all makes sense to someone, I'm sure, but you wouldn't want to spend time with him or her at a picnic. Don't try to make sense of all of it yourself. It just is what it is, which is about half of your wages up to the maximum. You will know for sure when you get your benefit-determination letter from your state.

It will be even clearer when the first check comes. You should expect to see it three weeks after you file. You do not get a benefit for the first week of your unemployment in most states; you have to be unemployed for the second week. The check arrives in the third. You have 52 weeks to draw out your 26 weeks of benefits, should you qualify for them.

If the unemployment rate is high enough in your area, you might be eligible for another 26 weeks of emergency benefits. Also, if your company sent your job out of the country or closed a plant, you may qualify for additional benefits. The Trade Readjustment Assistance program covers some laid-off workers by providing additional weeks of unemployment benefits and training dollars. Be sure to find out if your layoff is covered by this program.

To help you read the charts in the appendixes, I feel compelled to give you a lesson in Department of Labor-ese. It's a little-known language that you may find otherwise-understandable people speaking to you during this process. You won't always be able to find a translator when you need one, so review this quick reference guide: ·

- **wba: weekly benefit amount.** The amount of money they pay you before taxes.
- **BP: base period.** The four of the five calendar quarters prior to your layoff that they use to determine your eligibility and benefits.

- **bpw: base period wages.** The amount of money you earned in your base period.

- **HQ: high quarter.** The calendar quarter during your base period when you earned the most money.

- **hqw: high quarter wages.** The amount of money you earned in your high quarter.

- **aaw: average annual wage.** Your bpw divided by the number of weeks worked.

- **aww: average weekly wage.** Your average weekly earnings during your base period.

- **BY: benefit year.** The 52 weeks from the date you file from which you have to draw out your 26 weeks of benefit payments.

- **CQ: calendar quarter.** The three-month periods beginning with January, April, July, and October.

- **CY: calendar year.** The 12 months beginning in January.

- **dep: dependent.** People you claim on your unemployment insurance application. (different than for ies)

- **da: dependent allowance.** An additional benefit you might receive if you have dependents.

The day you applied, your benefit year began. Your weekly benefit may not begin right away if you have received any final payments from your employer, such as vacation pay or severance bonuses. If you have a good relationship with your employer, you can ask her to report those final payments as happening in the last week of your employment. She will get a form that must be returned within 10 days in which she indicates her treatment of these payments. This is her option and will allow your benefits to begin immediately. If she chooses to report them as being paid out over weeks or months, then your benefits will begin when your payments from her end, unless they are less than your weekly benefit amount.

Allowing you to receive these benefits may impact your employer's future unemployment premium rates, so they may be reluctant, especially if they are trying to hold onto a struggling business. Employers have a balance on account with their unemployment compensation coverage. That balance goes up with premiums paid in, and down with benefits paid out. If it goes down far enough, their premium rate goes up. The employer is not penalized directly for having a claim against them, but eventually they will pay it back into their account.

Another issue that can impact your benefits is retirement-fund distributions. If you take any retirement funds as cash, they will be counted against you in the process to determine your benefits. If you roll them over to another tax-deferred investment, they will not affect your unemployment benefits. Also, loans that must be retired at separation will not affect your benefits. If you know that there is no other option for you than to use your 401(k) funds during your layoff period, you would be better off to borrow them out before you are laid off or to wait until your unemployment benefits are exhausted to cash them out.

A very big question on everyone's mind when they get laid off is whether they should seek part-time work to make ends meet while searching for a career position. Income from part-time work will affect your benefit calculation. Would you be totally surprised if I told you that every state does this differently, too? Find your state in Appendix 5.5 to see how much you can make before they start taking away dollars. It probably isn't much. Unless you can make significantly more than your weekly benefit, you are probably better off aggressively searching for full-time employment. It should be noted that other family members can make more money during your period of unemployment and it won't affect your benefits.

And just when you thought this was getting easy, we have to talk about taxes. Amazing, but true, you have to pay income tax on your unemployment benefits. The government gets you coming or going, and you didn't pay tax on the premium, so you get to pay tax on the benefit. You won't pay Social Security tax on it, however, and therefore it won't count into your benefit calculations with that program when you retire.

If you are out of work for a short period and your tax bracket "is up there," you could end up owing over a third of your benefit check back to one or another government. You have the option of asking for the federal taxes to be withheld, but they will be withheld at the lowest rate. You will need to pay the difference as quarterly estimates, extra withholding at your next job, or a payment when you file next April. You will also need to remember that these same options apply to your state and city taxes, because the unemployment compensations folks won't withhold them for you. They're busy, and now you understand why.

It may be a blessing that no government has mandated withholding. You may choose to take the entire benefit amount and pay the taxes later. That's perfectly acceptable. It will be important to keep this in mind as you ask your next employer to withhold taxes. The easiest way to repay this obligation is to overwithhold on your next income. You could also have your spouse increase withholding on his or her check. This is a no-interest debt, but one with a pretty quick repayment period. So be very careful.

MY BEST ADVICE

Try to get your employer to report any severance pay as happening the week of your separation, and don't take any distributions from your 401(k) plan until you have used up your unemployment benefits. Try to have other family members work more while you pick up their unpaid responsibilities, to minimize the impact on your benefits.

Appeals

The unemployment compensation system has an extensive system of appeals that you are entitled to access, should you have a claim disallowed for a reason that you disagree with. At each level you will have two to three weeks to request the next appeal. Make sure you meet the deadline on your decision or you may be out of luck.

In most states you will find the following levels:

- **Redetermination.** An administrative appeal within the agency that handles the applications. This is like asking for a supervisor to look at it for you. It gets more attention from a more highly trained individual and may solve your problem.

- **Lower Level Appeal.** A hearing at the agency or a Review Commission or Board that is a separate agency from the one you were fighting with. You will be given an opportunity to talk with a hearing officer in person or over the phone and tell your side of the story. Have your witnesses and documents ready. You will rarely be given another hearing. Your employer will be there, too.

- **Higher Level Appeal.** An appeal to an administrative judge panel at the Review Commission or Board. The panel will review your request for further appeal. If granted, you may have a second hearing with a hearing officer or a panel.

- **An appeal to your local courts.** This might require an attorney and will take some time. You may get another week to file this one.

If you have been laid off and your employer is not contesting that fact, the most common reasons you may find yourself needing to appeal include the following:

- Those pesky final payments from your employer that prevent you from getting benefits.

- Your refusal to accept an offer of employment. This is where that debate about suitability would start again.

- Your lack of job-seeking activity.

If your employer is the one who is appealing your claim, remember that you can appeal any decision that goes against you. You can always take it to the next level.

MY BEST ADVICE

If you need to appeal, meet the deadlines, follow the rules, and show up at the hearings. It is not a hard process to follow if you read the really little print on everything they send you.

What You Should Know by Now

1. Whether or not you qualify for unemployment benefits.
2. Approximately how much your weekly benefit will be.
3. How to apply for benefits.
4. Where the nearest One-Stop Center is to you for other services.
5. What you need to do to have your benefits continue.
6. What events might reduce or eliminate your benefits.
7. How you will handle the income taxes on your benefits.
8. How to appeal your claim, if necessary.

Next Steps

1. _____
2. _____
3. _____
4. _____
5. _____
6. _____
7. _____
8. _____

6

Your Transition Budget

I'm going to assume for the sake of this chapter that budgeting is not the sport that you lettered in during high school. Even if you worked with numbers in your job, the numbers at home look very different. For starters, they have a lot fewer zeroes after them. But the real difference is that the numbers at work represent money that isn't yours.

The numbers at home represent much more than just money. They represent your lifestyle and all the financial decisions that you have made up to this point. When you made those decisions, you had a job and an income and an expectation that that income would continue for some indefinite period of time. Had you known that your job was going to end when it did, you would have made different decisions. Your gut reaction to your layoff may be to try to figure out which of those decisions you need to reverse.

How to Adjust Expenses

Given that the income stream you were counting on has changed, it's important to understand that all of the decisions you will be making in the next few days and weeks are transitional or short-term decisions. Remember that you're going to be doing something else in the near future, and that it will likely bring with it new income. That new income will either be less than, equal to, or more than your previous income from your recent employment. When you learn which it will be, then is the time to make any permanent adjustments in your lifestyle.

Even if your transition period continues to the point, for instance, when you will need to sell your home, you can still think of that decision as a transitional decision, renting for a while until your income returns to the point where you can afford to be a homeowner again. A permanent decision to sell your home and not return to homeownership would follow from a permanent reduction in income. One of the biggest mistakes that people make who are experiencing any form of financial difficulty is to mismatch a solution with a problem. Make sure that you apply short-term solutions to short-term problems and long-term solutions to long-term problems.

One of the most useless and insulting concepts in the field of financial planning is the use of the terms "wants" and "needs." Last time I checked, I believe that all humans need is to take a breath every couple of minutes, have some water every couple of days, and some food every couple of weeks, and we can keep going. Everything beyond that is a want.

Or we could take the opposite approach and define absolutely everything that you purchase as a need; because, at the moment that you purchased it, you justified to yourself in some way that you needed it. Of the thousands of families in my financial counseling practice, no one has ever walked into my office and declared that they were buying things that were extra. Because, by definition, if they bought them, they included them in a category of things that weren't extra. The things they left in the store were extra.

So let's just agree that with the exception of a minimal amount of air, water, food, and protection from the elements, everything is extra. But that doesn't mean that you don't need it or that you won't need to keep paying for it, because you've entered into an installment contract that will be reported unfavorably on your credit report if you stop.

The best way to approach this is to start with whatever you have in your lifestyle, and consider those things as ground zero. Ask yourself these questions:

- Could I, for a short period of time, find a way to spend less money on that expense?
- Could I do it less often?
- Could I do it at a less expensive location?
- Could I find a way to gain the same benefit but spend less money?

Remember, these are temporary reductions. Don't eliminate something you know will cost you even more to add back to your budget later. Food is the easiest area of your budget to practice this with. In taking a simple example of potatoes, you can see how this strategy works. You could take the routine purchase of a serving of french fries from the drive-thru and reduce it to a bag of frozen french fries from the grocery store. Then reduce that to a bag of fresh potatoes that you fry up yourself. You could take it another step and eliminate the cost of the oil and bake the potato. Then you could reduce the cost of running the oven for an hour by using the microwave. What you have done is eliminate the cost of the convenience and the labor costs inherent in making that potato ready for you to eat as a french fry.

Most people can live a week or two, even a month or two, without french fries from a fast-food restaurant. You might decide during that month or two that you don't like them that much, anyway, but only purchased them because they're easy. After the month, you find that you're not buying them as much any more. Or you might be very aware of the fact that they're missing from your life and you add them back right away when your income returns. Either way, the initial decision to reduce your expenditure on french fries in your budget is a lot easier if you see it as a short-term decision. You might even find that discovering alternative ways to enjoy your french fries without spending as much money can actually be empowering.

All these little decisions add up to feeling more in control of your financial well-being. You can choose to think of these decisions as deprived responses to a devastating situation. But, you have the choice to frame these decisions as positive, clever actions that are keeping you in control of a situation that feels very out of control in many ways.

If you don't know where your money goes during normal times, now would be a really good time to find out. The chart in Appendix 6.1 is an easy way to separate your budget into four categories. We will talk more about the split between bills and debts in Chapter 9, "Credit Issues." For now, if it has interest, it is a debt. Cash expenditures are frequent and predictable. Periodic expenditures are less frequent and less predictable. In a real budget, we would be averaging these expenses over the long run. For your purposes today, think about what you will need to spend, on the average, in the next 60 to 90 days.

The problem is that if you didn't track your expenses when times were good, you're probably not going to like doing it much right now. Becoming conscious about your spending is the important part, regardless of whether or not you choose to write down your expenses. If writing down your expenses helps to bring you a sense of control and gives you more information from which to plan, then by all means, do it. If, however, writing down your expenses causes you more stress because you can't remember to do it or because it merely reminds you more often of an altogether bad situation, then don't do it.

There are ways to monitor and control spending without formal budget charts. One way that makes you more aware of where your money's going is to spend only cash. Especially if you received any severance, bonuses, or vacation pay or you have cashed out any retirement funds, it's going to be difficult to know what's affordable.

If you were to put yourself on a weekly allowance to take care of ongoing expenses, this might be the only number that you have to track. If you don't have any lump sums you're working from right now and your income stream has been diminished, then it will be essential that you choose some system like this. Continuing the same schedule of your earlier paydays, cash out a specific amount of cash to last until the next payday. What this does is reduce your decision-making to that one-week or two-week period, and gives you an automatic sense of how long your money will last.

This strategy also helps to prevent a common challenge among people who need to temporarily reduce their lifestyle. Many times they will overcompensate and reduce too much, causing periodic binges, which actually set them back more than if they had set a more realistic weekly expenditure level.

MY BEST ADVICE

Put yourself on a cash budget with the same schedule as your previous paydays. Staying within the cash you have allocated, look for ways to maintain your same enjoyment of life with fewer expenses.

Sources of Supplemental Income

You may find that temporary supplemental income is a good strategy for balancing your budget while you're designing the best career move. You may find that your next career position will be at less income than you're used to, and rather than cut your lifestyle, you would prefer to supplement that income while you wait out the time that it will take for your income to rebound. Or you may know that the number of jobs available in your field has been reduced due to some economic forces and that you would rather wait out that cycle working in an unrelated job.

Since job-seeking itself is a full-time job, it's difficult to maintain what will be a second full-time job unless you are very clever with your schedule. Chances are you will want to keep some daytime hours available to return phone calls and to interview for your career position. Your supplemental income, therefore, will need to come from a job with either a very flexible schedule or one which allows those daytime hours to be free. Job-seeking not only takes a lot of time, it also takes a lot of creativity and energy. This is where your focus needs to be right now, so your supplemental income should come from activities that require very little creativity and less energy than you might spend in a career position.

We will talk later in the book about using your current separation from your previous job as an opportunity to begin a business. If that appeals to you, then that should become your sole focus. We'll discuss how to know whether that's a good idea for your situation in Chapter 15, "Business Opportunities."

Again, I would not recommend starting a small business with the idea that it is a side business intended to provide supplemental income. At first glance, direct sales and other work-from-home opportunities may look as though they provide the flexibility and the extra income that you need right now. The energy and excitement that surrounds many of the recruiting efforts of these companies will seem very appealing to a person who's just been released from employment. They add back camaraderie and self-esteem that may be missing.

In most situations, they actually do the opposite. They drain resources from an already-tight budget and they require more creativity and energy than it may seem when you're investigating them. Unless you intend to make this business opportunity your full-time venture, in most cases it will prove to be counterproductive. Learning a new business takes a lot of energy and a lot of concentration. Your energy and concentration need to be focused on securing your next career position. Don't lose sight of that important goal.

So what kind of opportunities do make good jobs to supplement your income during this time period? The best answer is anything that seems fun to you. You'll be spending much of your day doing activities that will not seem very fun. If you can balance that with a job that you always wanted to do or an activity that you did once as a youth and found pleasant, that's a great place to start.

Think about your hobbies and your vacations. What do you like to do the most? Do you like to be around people? Do you like to be off by yourself? Do you like to work with details? Are you better with the big picture? There's something that you always wanted to learn how to do, and working in that environment might bring you closer to that goal.

Another way to think about supplemental income is to look at your expenses and determine which of them you could reduce by working in that area. For instance, if you worked two days a week at your child's day care center, you might be able to trade off a lower cost for their care the rest of the week. Stocking shelves at your local grocer might give you an employee discount for the food that you buy. Doing the books for your car mechanic might keep your car running during this crucial time. Or teaching a class at the local college might get your kids some cheap credits next summer.

Just as we thought about how to match the term of the problem with the term of the change in expenses, you'll want to do the same with supplemental income. There are a lot of jobs that would drive you crazy, especially if you felt you would be doing them for the rest of your life. But knowing that you have a four- or five-month stint while you determine where your next career position is makes it a little more tolerable.

If, however, you know that you can't reenter the job market at the salary that you previously enjoyed, then you may have to supplement your income in order to stay in your field. In this case, you'll really be looking for something that does balance your work life and add value to your day. Friends and the Internet will probably be your best sources of information on where to locate this temporary job. You're not looking for perfection here; you're looking for cash. And it's perfectly okay to accept a job that you know may not be exactly what you're looking for, because by the time you find that perfect job, you might not need it any more.

Other sources of supplemental income can be derived from different assets that you own. Up to now we've been talking about the asset of your time and your talent, but you may be able to generate an income from other assets. Spending your accumulated investment capital is your last resort, and spending capital that has been tax deferred comes after that. But restructuring the income flow from those investments might provide you the money that you need during this time. For instance, you may own a mutual fund that automatically reinvests its dividends; if, instead, you took those dividends in cash, that would provide you some additional income. Or, you might own a mutual fund that is growth-oriented and doesn't generate much cash income. Repositioning that investment into a fund that does pay income would be a solution. Financial planners are used to coaching their clients through these decisions at retirement. You could view your temporary unemployment as an early retirement period during which you need to take some of the same strategies and apply them to your situation.

Other tangible assets may also have income-generating possibilities. If you have an extra bedroom in your home or apartment, you might be able to generate cash by renting it to someone. Students are probably the best place to start since they are also looking for temporary housing. Again, we're matching the term of the problem with the term of the solution. Think about other assets that you own that you might rent or lease to someone who has a short-term need. Use Appendix 6.2 to compare all your sources of supplemental income.

Now would be a great time to get rid of items that you no longer use or that are too expensive to maintain. You now have access to buyers virtually everywhere via the online sites such as e-Bay and Craigslist. If you haven't been to one of these sites, I would suggest you hang out there for a little bit to see the types of things that people are selling. You may have all kinds of treasures hidden in your basement, attic, or garage that others might be willing to pay money for. Garage sales are a nice opportunity as well to make money on things that don't have as much of a specific market. Throwing out old things is also wonderfully therapeutic and consistent with the notion that you are moving on to a new phase of your career-life. If you can surround yourself at home with a sense of newness and control, this will contribute to an overall sense of well-being.

If you are one of the laid-off workers who has been offered a severance package that includes ongoing income, you may not need to address the need for supplemental income for a number of months. You might take this opportunity, however, to earn some additional income, to retire some debts, or pay some large expenses so that your overall need for income is reduced as you search for suitable reemployment. If you take the edge off a stressed budget, it will allow you more freedom in your job-search and more options as to the positions you can accept.

Maybe the hardest type of severance income to manage is that which comes as a lump sum. You may have received some accumulated vacation or sick pay, or you may have received a one-time payment. We are always tempted to take those lump sums and pay off an irritating bill, or purchase a new computer, or do something else that seems justified at the time in our quest for a new job. You shouldn't look at this lump sum payment as a windfall. Instead, think of it as a source of supplemental income. If you place it in a money market account and draw it down on paydays, it will enable you to maintain the same cash flow as when you were employed. Then calculate how long that lump sum will supplement any other income you have right now and enable you to maintain the same lifestyle.

Even though paying off the credit card may seem to alleviate stress, it's possible that you would be paying an amount that wouldn't come due until after you were reemployed. So you are diverting precious money that should be used for short-term needs into a long-term purpose. However, if you have a debt that would be retired anyway within the time period that this money will last, it would be a good idea to go ahead and pay it off because you will save a little bit of interest.

Other family members, your spouse, children, or parents living with you may have income coming into the household already or may offer to seek additional income during this time period.

They may also offer to pick up a certain bill or expense for the family while you're unemployed, which amounts to the same thing as increasing your income.

The hard part comes in when the teenager decides that he's paying the cable bill because that's his highest priority in the household budget. Your real-world situation dictates that cable is unaffordable for a while. This is a good lesson for a teenager to participate in. Helping him understand that the money he would be paying toward the cable should really go toward paying the electric bill is a good way to help him begin to understand the constant choices that households must make in budgeting. The blatant reality is that if you don't have electricity, you don't watch cable anyway; this is a great example of the difficult choices that households must make when income declines.

Everyone in the family has different priorities for how money should be spent. The temporary cash-flow crunch is a wonderful time to help people learn to communicate positively and effectively about coordinating those various needs. Unfortunately, however, it also turns into a time when previously petty arguments turn into full-out wars, and the frustration over the layoff turns into guilt and shame to be used as weapons.

MY BEST ADVICE

As you seek out sources of supplemental income, remember that your primary full-time job is seeking your next career position. Make sure that you reserve your prime-time energy and creativity for that activity.

Dealing with Transitional Expenses

As you get used to the reality that you've been laid off, you'll notice that finding your next career position is going to cost you some money. There's just no way around it. With each of the expenses you incur, you can apply the same principles that we discussed, which will help with your ongoing expenses. List all expenses you will have in Appendix 6.3 and think about how to fund them.

There are four basic ways to pay for these expenses:

1. Take money from the current cash flow.
2. Spend your windfalls or emergency fund.
3. Go into debt.
4. Receive them as gifts.

The first option is usually the most stressful. If you believe that you can afford them out of current cash flow, but don't specifically identify the expenses that you can reduce, what you'll find is that you'll cause bills to become late. This will add to the stress of the job search. Spending from a windfall or from accumulated savings is probably the best option, because this type of expense is exactly what emergency funds are intended for. Going into debt on a low-interest credit card that may not need to be repaid in full until after you're working would be a second option worth considering.

Gifts from friends and relatives are also a nice way to fund them. Many times, people have an interest in helping you through a temporary setback and are unsure how to help. Gifts that involve funding the transitional expenses are very appropriate. They speak directly to the immediate need without taking away your sense of responsibility for maintaining your ongoing bills. A family member could, for instance, purchase some long distance cards to enable you to return phone calls, or could give you a gift certificate at a local print shop.

If your employer has not provided you with free outplacement services, you may require other services that will cost you money. We'll cover these in detail in Chapter 13, "Finding the Next Job."

MY BEST ADVICE

Even though the expenses of a job search are an investment in your future, you can still look for creative ways to keep them at a minimum.

Communication and Monitoring

Speaking with family members may be the last thing you want to do more of right now. Especially with those whom you feel you've let down or who may be judging you. But the success of any transitional budget is going to rest on the predictable and positive communication patterns that you establish with all of the people who are sharing in the income and the expenses of the budget.

Nobody likes surprises. You can attest to that as you've just been through a very bad surprise. The more you share with your family, the more they can respond appropriately and help to adjust as needs arise. If you don't tell them the whole story, they will fill in the blanks, and they may fill them in wrong. This will lead to feelings of mistrust and insecurity, which is exactly what you don't need your family feeling at this moment.

Set a time each week when all of you can gather and catch up on the week's activities. You might recap the different bills and expenses that have come in that week. What was paid, what is due to be paid. You can bring them up-to-date on your job-search activities, and the successes and disappointments you've had. And you can get their ideas on how to keep the household productive and thriving. Appendix 6.4 gives you a sample agenda to follow.

You'll be surprised at how creative children will be when presented with accurate information. Many parents feel that sharing this type of information with their children puts the burden on them. The reality is that they know whether you tell them or not, and it's much better for them to hear it straight from you with compassion and reassurance. It gives them time to readjust to any change that may be coming down the line. It keeps them from acting out in ways that might wind up costing you even more money.

Have everyone who is involved decide on some sort of a system in which everyone can access information. In some households, the computer is where the checkbook and other financial data are stored, but one or more members of the household don't have the computer skills to read it. Try to find a way, such as a journal or a notebook, which gives everyone the ability to keep on top of the current situation. They may never look at it, but knowing that they can will take away much of the anxiety that they feel about the transition period.

MY BEST ADVICE

The more information that family members have, the more creative and supportive they can be. Keeping them out of the loop also keeps them out of the solution.

What You Should Know by Now

1. If you want to track expenses by using an expense journal or other written budgeting tool.

2. If you'd rather use a cash-only system that manages your cash flow as you go.

3. If your budget needs supplemental income while job-hunting.

4. What sources of supplemental income you would find acceptable.

5. How much supplemental income other family members can generate for the household.

6. What transitional expenses you will have, and how to minimize them.

7. How you are going to communicate on a regular basis with all family members about your joint financial situation.

8. Where you are going to store financial information so that everyone who is involved in the problem-solving process can access it.

Next Steps

1. ———————————————————————
2. ———————————————————————
3. ———————————————————————
4. ———————————————————————
5. ———————————————————————
6. ———————————————————————
7. ———————————————————————
8. ———————————————————————

7

Insurance Decisions

If you're like most working Americans, you have been relying heavily on your employer to purchase various insurance products on your behalf. You may now be caught short without those policies that you have come to depend on. After a layoff, some policies will be able to be converted to individual polices, some will continue for a time as group policies, and some will just go away. If you are healthy and insurable, you get to go shopping and learn what the market values are for the coverage that you currently need.

If, however, you have experienced any serious health crisis, usually in the last five years, then most insurance companies will not be interested in doing business with you except at much higher rates or with unacceptable restrictions. It's unbelievable, but some employers' costs of providing the employee benefits is 40 or even 50 percent of your gross wages. This is money that is sometimes invisible to you because it does not show up on your pay stub. Once you lose the benefits that went with those dollars, however, it will be very noticeable.

Health Insurance

In many corners of the country, the term "good benefits" is virtually synonymous with group health insurance. All the other benefits that the employer pays for are just extras. The health insurance payment systems that go along with our health care delivery industry are in a state of turmoil. Premiums are rising at two or three times the annual inflation rate. More and more people are operating without health insurance to protect their families. While the politicians, hospitals, doctors, pharmaceutical companies, and insurance carriers duke this one out, you're left needing to make an important decision.

Along with the other changes your family will experience in the near term, changing doctors or getting used to a new system of payment seems like an added burden. If you are laid off in the middle of the month, you will normally be covered until the last calendar day of that month on your company's group policy. Then you'll need to make a determination of whether you will be using your option to continue that coverage and pay the premium yourself. This is afforded you by a law that we refer to as COBRA (Consolidated Omnibus Budget Reconciliation Act). This law covers employers with over 20 employees. Many states have "mini-COBRA" laws that require employers with fewer than 20 employees to continue your coverage at your cost.

If your employer was paying a significant portion of your premium, you'll go through true sticker shock when you see what the premium will be that you'll be expected to pay. You'll receive this option for 18 months. You're allowed to change plans within the same options that the company offers their employees. You must pay the premium to your employer in advance of the month for which you desire coverage, and many employers now use third-party administrators to collect these payments. The coverage and the relationship with your doctors should continue uninterrupted, and the only changes that you will see in your policy should be the changes that affect all employees of the company.

If you and the members of your family are all relatively healthy, you may find it advantageous to shop for your own coverage. Several insurance companies offer temporary policies, which you purchase by the day. For example, you can purchase coverage for 30 days, 90 days, or 180 days. When those days are over, the policy expires. Some companies allow you to purchase another number of days for a similar premium. The risk is that you may not be insurable when that policy expires, and therefore may be prohibited from purchasing another one. Any claims or illnesses ongoing when the policy expires will continue to be paid, but the long-term security from these policies is not there. These are obviously policies that are intended to bridge a gap between one group policy and the next. They are very affordable, and they normally give you access to the doctors that you are used to seeing, but they won't cover any costs for care on preexisting conditions.

Blue Cross/Blue Shield affiliates, United Healthcare, Aetna and other insurance companies also sell permanent individual policies, which you might find more cost-effective because you have options, such as higher deductibles, that can limit the cost to your family. There are many online sites that allow you to compare prices and provisions, but a local health insurance broker can guide you quickly to the best option.

In most states, you can join health maintenance organizations (HMO) as an individual. If you are not insurable, they have open enrollment months when they cannot ask medical questions to screen potential members. You may find their rates as high as and sometimes higher than your COBRA option.

There is an option, which is attractive to some, called a Health Savings Account (HSA). Offered through insurance agents and brokers, you purchase a family policy with an extremely high deductible, from \$2,200 to \$10,000, and you deposit into a tax-free savings account the remainder of what you would have paid in a premium if you had chosen a lower deductible. You can deposit up to a maximum determined each year (\$5,950 for 2009). This money, from the savings account, is then available to you to pay the smaller claims that your family may encounter. If you have relatively low claims, then that money is not lost. It rides in the account and is yours to spend in later years. This is a way to split the risk between yourself and the insurance company and possibly come out ahead in the long run.

COBRA is a program that you must get into under a very strict deadline, but you can opt out of it any time you want. The other plans that you might find can be picked up at some point when you determine that you are eligible for them and that they serve your needs. Your state's insurance commissioner can provide you with a list of insurance companies licensed to sell health insurance in your state. Check out your state's website and toll-free number in Appendix 7.1.

MY BEST ADVICE

Wait until near the deadline to fill out all the paperwork required to participate in your COBRA plan while you are investigating other options that might be available and attractive to you.

Life Insurance

Your need for life insurance is determined by the answers to the following two questions:

1. Will anyone benefit financially by your continued existence?

2. Will anyone suffer financially from your demise?

If the answer to either of these is yes, then you have a need for life insurance to make sure that either that benefit continues past your death or that the suffering is minimized at your death.

The amount you need also stems from the answers to those two questions.

1. How much will a person benefit financially by your continued existence, and how much money would it take to fund that benefit?

2. What would the financial suffering be, and how much insurance would it take to reduce or eliminate that suffering?

Compare your answers to the amount of insurance you hold separately from your employer's plan to get an idea of how much you need to replace. If you are healthy and insurable, you can pick up a quick term insurance policy for a few dollars a month. If you are not healthy or insurable, you may need to consider converting some or all of the coverage that your employer carried on you into an individual policy. Be aware that these premiums will be relatively high because the insurance companies aren't dumb, and they know that only unhealthy people will opt for this conversion.

If you're not sure about your insurability, then my advice would be to go ahead and convert your group life insurance into an individual policy while you apply for and determine your eligibility for an individual policy that you purchase elsewhere. I would apply these same questions and analysis to any coverage that you carried on your spouse or your children through your employer.

Once you are reemployed, you can once again compare the benefits available from your new employer, and you may choose to drop the term policies that you've picked up for this interim period. But, you may also choose to forego the new employer's coverage and maintain your individual polices. This would guarantee your coverage should you be laid off again.

MY BEST ADVICE

Don't assume that the amount of life insurance your employer provided was the exact amount you needed. Replace it if you need it, buy more if it wasn't enough, or buy less if it was too much.

Disability Insurance

This is a tough one, so read carefully. Your level of disability coverage is the most important factor in maintaining your family's financial security. It is equally important through your period of unemployment. This is the coverage that ensures you will have an income should you become disabled and are prevented from returning to gainful employment. Let me repeat: Your level of disability coverage is the most important factor in maintaining your family's financial security.

As much as you worry about how you will continue your health insurance, you should be worrying twice as much about continuing your disability insurance. Most group plans are convertible to individual policies, but most people don't ask to do this so their benefits departments may not be giving them the same level of information as they provide regarding COBRA. When you ask for the information, you may find that:

1. Your waiting period may be longer.
2. Your benefit period may be shorter.
3. Your premium may be higher.

4. Certain causes of disability may be excluded.

5. The definition of disability may be more narrow.

Since this is a temporary solution to a temporary problem, I wouldn't be annoyed by these changes. Think of it as your "COBRA" for disability insurance. You won't be keeping that policy forever either. However, if you choose self-employment as your next career strategy, this may be the only disability policy you will qualify for until you have three years of consistent income.

If your group policy won't convert, essentially, you're just stuck without this type of insurance until you get another job. You'll be covered by Social Security Disability for a short time, depending on how long you have worked in Social Security–covered employment. But the very purpose of private disability insurance is to replace lost income. Since you currently have no earned income, you can't replace it. Even though a disability at this moment would possibly eliminate future income, there is no insurance company that will sell you an individual disability policy right now.

This is a rather obscure reason to grab any old job you can find, especially one that isn't very physically risky and doesn't offer you disability insurance as a group benefit. At that point you could purchase an individual policy and have at least some coverage in the event you become disabled before any new group policy kicks in at your next career employer.

However, if you have the slightest history of health concerns, like a nagging back or a bout of depression a year ago, the insurance company probably won't sell you a policy. So like I said, you're sort of stuck. This is the real health insurance crisis in our country that no one is paying attention to.

MY BEST ADVICE

While you are uninsured, be really careful. Don't do anything stupid. Eliminate a good part of the risk yourself by avoiding potentially disabling situations.

Workers' Compensation Insurance

If you haven't suffered a job related injury or illness recently, you probably didn't even think about this one as being something you just lost. Even so, your employer was paying into a state fund or privately administered insurance fund, which covered you in the event you were hurt on the job. It would have paid medical expenses and reimbursed lost income so that your employer would not be directly liable for these expenses. Your benefits should continue in most cases after a layoff if you have an active claim. Also, each state has a statute of limitations for new claims relating to injuries at previous employers.

As many unemployed individuals do, you might be picking up side work, or contract work, or other forms of self-employed activity. You might also have already established a side business or be thinking about doing that. Especially if you're thinking about becoming self-employed on a permanent basis, one of the first things that you should do is establish yourself in the workers' compensation pool in your state. You can call their office and receive a number which qualifies you as someone participating in the plan. Find your state's agency in Appendix 7.2.

In most states, you pay the premium after-the-fact, based on the payroll that you incurred during that premium period. So usually, the cost of just being in the system is negligible and, if you never do any contract work and are immediately rehired, it hasn't cost you very much. If you are doing any work and receiving any money, the premium should also be fairly small. It will also cover anyone that you invite to do the work with you. It will help you to limit your liability on their injuries.

This will provide you some level of health and disability insurance for the times that you're providing services for other people. Even if you are carrying an individual disability policy, workers' compensation can provide you an added layer of security. Your benefits from your private policy will not be reduced if you also receive benefits from your workers' compensation coverage. This differs from Social Security disability benefits, which will reduce coverage from your individual policy. Your workers' compensation will also pay the first dollars on work-related medical expenses that might otherwise be included in a deductible or co-payment on your health insurance. It also pays partial disability benefits that many disability policies would not cover.

MY BEST ADVICE

Having workers' compensation coverage may be your only way to provide yourself some disability insurance while you are self-employed.

What You Should Know by Now

1. What coverage your previous employer provided for you.

2. Which of those coverages are convertible to individual policies.

3. How to cover yourself using the COBRA option on your group health insurance.

4. What other health insurance policies are available to you as an individual.

5. How much life insurance you need and whether you are insurable.

6. How to convert your life insurance to an individual policy, if needed.

7. How to purchase disability insurance if your next employer doesn't offer the coverage, and whether or not you are insurable.

8. How to join the workers' compensation pool in your state.

Next Steps

1. _____

2. _____

3. _____

4. _____

5. _____

6. _____

7. _____

8. _____

8

Retirement Decisions

We humans have developed some pretty keen survival instincts that don't serve us very well in our overall financial planning process. If your kid is about to run out into the street in front of an oncoming car, you have the ability to focus, saving that child from injury. You will forget, totally, for those few moments, that he spends most waking hours sitting in front of a computer playing video games, which will most likely cause him to develop heart disease before he's 60. Why on Earth would you worry about a heart attack that he's going to have 40 years from now when he's about to be hit by a car? You wouldn't.

We have a similar problem when it comes to caring about our retirement funds on the day that we just lost our job. Sometimes that chunk of money sitting there looks as if it's more important to help us solve a problem today rather than to let it ride and to maintain the prospect of a secure retirement later.

Defined Benefit Plans

A couple of years ago the scale tipped in the United States when more than half of the money invested in retirement plans was being held in Defined Contribution plans. Prior to that, the majority of the funds were held in Defined Benefit plans.

The difference is exactly as the names imply. The Defined Benefit plan *defines the benefit* you get out when you retire. The Defined Contribution plan *defines the contribution* that is put in for you each year. In each plan, the other item (benefit or contribution) is a variable.

In a Defined Benefit plan, each year your employer will be told by the actuaries how much to contribute into your pension fund. This will make sure that your benefits, which are usually *defined* as some multiple of your earnings, will be there for you to enjoy at retirement. Defined Benefit plans are expensive to establish and maintain. They have gone out of favor with many employers to the point that many workers under 40 have never been covered by one. The only way they would be familiar with them is if their mother or father is receiving a pension check from a previous employer.

So what happens to the money in your Defined Benefit plan when you leave the company? First of all, you're only entitled to this money if you've been there long enough to be what the government calls "vested." Vesting is calculated on a chart that tells you how long you have to be in a plan before you are entitled to certain percentages of the money that has been contributed on your behalf. In most plans, after five years you are fully vested. Some plans that were established long ago have longer vesting schedules.

You can usually do three things with your pension money from a Defined Benefit plan.

1. You can leave it in the pension fund with the company and take it as a pension benefit at your retirement date.

2. You can have the company deposit it directly into an IRA account for you. (This is called a rollover.)

3. You can have the company pay it to you in cash.

In the first two options, you will incur no current tax bill on the transaction. In the last, you will have 20 percent of the funds withheld by your employer and deposited with the federal government as a withholding tax payment. You will probably also be required to pay additional tax when you file your tax return the following year. The penalty for withdrawal is 10 percent, and the tax will be paid at your current tax bracket, which will probably be more than 10 percent, and so the 20 percent your employer withholds will come up short. This angers a lot of people because they falsely believe that the tax withheld from the distribution already paid their entire obligation.

All funds deposited into qualified pension plans are insured by the Pension Benefit Guarantee Corporation (PBGC), a federal agency. It operates similarly to the Federal Deposit Insurance Corporation (FDIC) in that it ensures that your money is safe if the company holding it goes out of business or otherwise mishandles it. Given that your company just laid you off, you may be concerned about their stability as a manager of your retirement funds. This feeling would be normal.

Probably the best way to ensure that those funds will be available for your retirement is to leave them in the pension fund. If you roll them over into an IRA, you will then have ongoing access to them to spend as an emergency fund. If you were already in a financial bind before the layoff, and you don't see any other means of getting through, then rolling them over into an IRA may be your best solution. You could then cash them out if you actually need them before you secure new income.

The tax rules, however, are complicated, and if you know that you will be spending all the money in one tax year, you might want to take the lump sum distribution directly from your employer and not park it in an IRA temporarily. Taking it as a lump sum preserves your option, in some cases, to spread those taxes out over the next 5 to 10 years. Your tax preparer can help you determine how these rules may apply to you.

One reason to leave your pension funds where they are is the possibility that you might return to this employer at some later date. The effects of years of service are cumulative and will add to your pension benefit at retirement. If you cash it out, you may not be able to buy back those earlier years when you return. You will have to start all over again on the vesting schedule.

MY BEST ADVICE

If you have the option to leave your Defined Benefit plan funds where they are, you will incur no tax penalties and continue to enjoy the insurance coverage provided by the Pension Benefit Guarantee Corporation.

Defined Contribution Plans

When Defined Contribution plans first started, they were a type of deferred compensation program that enabled your employer to pay you wages and to defer the date that you received them and, thus, defer the date that you had to pay taxes on them. About 30 years ago, a bright individual figured out that one interpretation of a previously unnoticed section of the IRS code could allow employees to choose to defer additional wages and pay the tax later. This, of course, was the 401(k) and 403(b) section of the IRS code.

It's become so popular that we now call Defined Contribution plans that use this option "401(k) plans," and we look at the employer's contribution as the afterthought. We talk about how much the employee can contribute and how much the employer will match of that contribution. It really doesn't matter whose money you call it. It's all the employee's money because it's created out of his or her productivity for the company. If you've worked at your company longer than a year, chances are you've begun participating in your 401(k) plan.

You will probably be given the same options as explained earlier for Defined Benefit plans.

1. You can leave it in the pension fund with the corporation, and take it as a pension benefit at your retirement date.

2. You can have the corporation deposit it directly in to an IRA account for you. (This is called a rollover.)

3. You can have them pay it to you in cash.

You will also have another decision, in some situations, if any amount of your company's plan is invested in their stock. Depending upon the conditions of your layoff, your company's stock may be worthless, or it may have just taken a big jump in the market because the corporate restructuring has been seen as positive by Wall Street analysts. If the company has a bright future without you, you may consider keeping it as stock or holding it until the price increases on the stock market. If the company is failing fast and may end up in receivership, then you, as a common stock holder, will be at the bottom of the barrel. You may want to cut your losses and cash it out right now. This is one of those lessons that many people learn the hard way. If you have a great deal of your assets in your company's stock, it is likely to be worth less at the moment that they lay you off and therefore not represent a good source of emergency funds.

As much as financial planners preach about not using retirement accounts as an emergency fund, many people still do. If you have an outstanding loan against your 401(k) plan, you are in a very difficult position at this time. Some companies will allow you to continue to make payments to them, which will be applied to the outstanding balance on your loan. But missing a payment causes a default, which results in tax consequences. If they don't offer you the option of continuing to make payments, then they will repay your loan with your existing funds balance, which will cause a taxable event. They will then withhold the 20 percent toward your taxes from the remainders of the money on account and pay the rest over to you, either in a rollover or a lump sum as you direct.

This is one of the biggest reasons not to take a loan against a 401(k) plan. But, again, it's hard to focus on longer-term consequences when short-term problems need to be solved. You may also find that the underlying value of the investments that secured that loan have gone down in value given the current economic climate during which you were laid off. This will affect your overall retirement planning significantly. You will need to revisit your retirement goals as soon as your income stabilizes, to determine how quickly you can get back on track. This might mean increasing future contributions to your plan or extending your retirement date.

MY BEST ADVICE

Know all your options regarding what you can do with your tax-deferred retirement funds. Minimize the tax consequences, and maximize the probability that this money will be there for its best purpose, your retirement.

Should You Retire Early?

Right up there with getting married, having a baby, and buying your first home, is the decision to retire. Many people spend an entire working lifetime preparing for that event. You might be in a position in which you've just been told that you have the option to retire earlier than you thought. Or you may have plenty of years in with your company, and this layoff is forcing your hand on a hard decision. You've got some thinking to do. The offer may include giving you the health insurance benefits available to retirees from your company and offering you a reduced monthly pension amount from the Defined Benefit plan. It might also offer you other life insurance and long-term care insurance benefits.

Locking in these added layers of security makes a lot of sense, even if you feel confident you will be reemployed with full benefits fairly soon. The reduced pension payments that you receive between now and your normal retirement date can be invested to supplement the reduced monthly payment past your retirement date. If you plan to seek and are fairly certain you will secure a full-time career position, you need to remember that your retirement income from your previous employer will be taxed at your tax bracket during your working years. For many individuals, that tax bracket will be lower after you stop working. This would be one reason to not accept the early retirement offer and to allow that money from your previous employer to continue to grow tax-free and be taxed later at a lower tax bracket.

Many times you must make this decision before many of these variables are known. So all you can do is make your best guess and weigh the risks of deciding one way or the other. If you don't take the retirement, you risk not being included in a health insurance plan if you don't secure a career position. If you do take the retirement offer and immediately secure a great job, your cost will be the additional taxes that you might pay by receiving your retirement benefits early.

The other half of this decision is whether you should actually retire and stop working. That decision will come from an analysis of your ability to support yourself on the income that the retirement benefit will provide. This may be a great opportunity to go do other projects or to start a business or even to change careers totally, by providing a reasonable income during that transition. I'd advise you not to become complacent just because you have income available to you. If you are not really ready to retire, yet you do not seek additional employment, you might be sorry 10 years down the road.

MY BEST ADVICE

If you take an early retirement benefit and continue working, invest your monthly income from your retirement benefit to supplement your income for the years when you really retire.

Should You Spend Any of Your Retirement Funds?

The short answer is no. The long answer is no, no, no. It may look appealing to take money from a 401(k) plan and pay off high-interest debt. What I have seen in my financial counseling practice is that the probability is high that you will continue to use high-interest vehicles to fund large purchases and then have no retirement fund.

If things have gotten to the point where you are considering declaring bankruptcy, and cashing out your pension funds will cause you to avoid that, then there may be some rationale. However, if it doesn't fix the problem entirely and you have to declare bankruptcy anyway, remember that your pension-plan funds were exempt from seizure in the bankruptcy proceeding as long as they were still in your employer's plan.

It might make more sense to reorganize your debts using a credit counselor or a Chapter 13 trustee than to sacrifice your retirement security. This, again, is a mismatch of the problem and solution. You're choosing a long-term solution to fix a short-term problem. And cashing out this money usually only delays by a month or two an inevitable decision, such as selling the home, moving, or getting a second job. Its tax-deferred status makes it the most powerful tool in your quest for financial security. Cashing it out is very expensive and you'll never regain what you've lost.

MY BEST ADVICE

Whatever financial pain you are going through, it is not as bad as the pain you will feel during retirement when you are missing this money. It is much better to suffer your consequences now, when you are young and healthy, than to try to find solutions when you are old and broke.

What You Should Know by Now

1. If your company has a Defined Benefit or a Defined Contribution plan or both.

2. How much your fund balances are in each, and if you are vested.

3. What options you have for the future of those funds.

4. What tax consequences you will encounter with each option.

5. What investment choices you prefer for a rollover.

6. How tempting it is to want to spend that money now.

7. What other choices you have for solutions to current cash-flow problems that don't involve spending that money.

8. How much you will need to increase your retirement fund contribution at your next employer if you have cashed out your current funds.

Next Steps

1. _____

2. _____

3. _____

4. _____

5. _____

6. _____

7. _____

8. _____

9

Credit Issues

Just like beauty, credit is in the eye of the beholder. But unlike beauty, it's a lot more than skin deep. It goes to the core of your values. It defines whether you're living in the past, the present, or the future. It says a lot about what kind of a risk-taker you are.

Unfortunately, your credit and the debt that you've accumulated as a result may be the tail wagging the dog in your financial decisions during your period of unemployment. Debt payments that seemed affordable when you were working full time may soon turn into the most annoying phone call of your day. Just as with other problems, however, there are many strategies for dealing with this issue. Let's look for the ones that will make the best sense for you.

Creditworthiness

For many years there was no such thing as a credit rating. Your credit was a snapshot of your contracts and your behavior with those contracts as compiled by a few credit-reporting agencies. With the advent of more powerful computers and more powerful antidiscrimination laws, many of these agencies started reducing this history to numbers as a convenience to their customers, the creditors, but these numbers were a secret. You, the consumer, didn't have access to them.

By 2000 Fair Isaacs had made a nice business out of calculating a number that ranked you against other debtors. Reducing your entire creditworthiness down to a single number is, of course, ridiculous. Most creditors will continue to apply their own standards and criteria to the decision of whether to extend you credit. But more and more of these evaluations have become standardized as they search for methods to make sure that they are complying with the antidiscrimination laws.

So then the question becomes, "What's a good score?" This, of course, is entirely up to the creditor. If they need to loan out $100 million a month to generate the profit that their stockholders are demanding, and they can only find enough people to loan out $90 million, they might be tempted to lower their standards. Likewise, if they have customers ready and willing to borrow $110 million, they could afford to be a little choosier with whom they do business.

Your credit score will never be an absolute statement of your worth as a human being. It is a statement of where you are in line with all the other potential customers who would like to do business with that creditor. This is very similar to the difference between having a 4.0 at your high school and being ranked in the ninety-fifth percentile of all high school students in the country on a specific exam. If the college you apply to fills its freshman class with people from the ninety-sixth percentile, it doesn't need you. Your 4.0 grade average doesn't matter.

So, it all depends upon whom you want to show this score to. Who are you likely to do business with in the future that will care? For instance, a bankruptcy may prevent you from leasing a car, but may not prevent you from securing a mortgage. This might not make any sense at first glance, because the car lease is probably going to be a much lower payment than the mortgage payment and a much shorter term than the term of the mortgage. But from the creditor's perspective, you put very little, if anything, down on a car lease and you can disappear with the car. Whereas, with a mortgage, you will be asked to put a substantial amount of cash down and they know where the house is. And therefore, they probably know where you are.

The extra security that the creditor receives in the form of a down payment and a tangible, unmovable asset enables them to overlook previous credit behavior that might be negative. They also might choose to increase your interest rate for a period of time until they feel you might be able to refinance with another company at a lower rate. At this point they will voluntarily lower the rate for you.

If you've always had what you considered perfect credit, you've enjoyed the freedom of never needing to have these conversations. And you will more than likely be able to keep it that way as you go through your period of unemployment. If your credit report, however, is nicked a little by some past problems, it will probably continue to show those problems, and you may accumulate a few more while you're unemployed.

Since income and length of employment are two very important criteria in assessing your creditworthiness, you will more than likely not be approved for certain types of loans during your unemployment period. If you find yourself needing to relocate and you currently own a home, you will probably have no problem securing a new mortgage in anticipation of your next source of income.

If, however, you find yourself needing to sell your home and relocate due to the affordability of your current housing, you may find that your credit report is very important. Landlords especially look at credit history very carefully. They not only care about your ability and willingness to pay your rent on time, they also care about how well you will take care of their property. To them, your credit report might be an indication of your level of responsibility with their property.

Even though it's complicated, it's still the best plan to try to maintain your credit standing as best you can. I would not make it your number one priority before housing and feeding your family, but I would consciously make every effort to minimize any marks that will need explaining in the future.

Negative information can be distributed about you for seven years after that account is closed. If an account is still open, chances are that creditor does not report an entire seven years of activity. They might report 36 or 48 months of activity. It states this on your report. If you have a late payment today on a credit card, in 48 months it would no longer be showing. If, however, you pay off that account and close it three months from now, that last report that they send in will stay on your file for seven years. Many times it's in your best interest to keep open accounts, even ones that you're not using, because the bad information will cycle off more quickly.

Be aware that an item is not reported to the credit reporting agency as late until it is 30 days past due. If your credit card statement says your payment is due on the second of May, you'll get a late fee on the third of May, but it won't be reported as late until the second of June. Many times, when people are short on cash, they find themselves making payments late and imagining that their credit report looks awful. When they finally see it, and those payments aren't showing up as late, they feel like they got away with something. They didn't. They just didn't understand the system.

It's always a good idea to look at your credit report from each of the three major credit-reporting agencies listed in Appendix

9.1 at least once a year. As an unemployed person, if you are currently seeking employment, you qualify for free reports from all three credit bureaus. The 1999 amendments to the Fair Credit Reporting Act made this possible. You must send in your requests in writing and state that you are unemployed and seeking employment.

Once you get your reports, you can review them for accuracy. I would suggest you put this on a list of things to do once you're back at work. Make sure you do it annually to keep up with any errors or problems that may show up. You have enough to be mad about right now. Getting mad about errors on your credit report isn't a positive activity to move you forward.

MY BEST ADVICE

Relax a little and put your creditworthiness in the category of important but not critical. Keep it in perspective as you work through the many other decisions you face right now.

Debt Management

Reexamining your priorities is not a bad thing. We all do it every time there is a significant change in our lives. Getting out of school, getting married, and having your first child all brought out some soul-searching and discussion about what was really important to you. Not-so-happy events like divorce, death, and the one you're living through now also prompt the same analysis. If you've worked and reworked your budget, and you've got a plan for making sure that each debt payment will be paid on time, that's marvelous. I encourage you to stick with the plan and minimize the amount of collateral damage that your layoff might cause.

I would suggest, however, that this is not the time to be paying any additional amounts on your debts. You may have had a goal of getting out of debt in a certain number of months. I would suggest that you take the additional money that you might be spending on retiring that debt early, and place it in an emergency fund until you're reemployed. At that point, you could take that money, and go ahead and apply it to the debt. You won't be that far behind, but you also will have it as an additional cushion should you need to make a payment that you can't afford down the road.

A temptation people have when they become unemployed is to take any final lump-sum payments from their employer and pay off a debt. I would advise the same strategy. Place that money in a savings account. Once you're employed, if you still want to pay off the debt, the money will be there to do it. But if your unemployment period runs longer that you anticipate, then you'll have that money to keep your cash flow going.

I would never recommend taking tax-deferred funds and using them to retire debts. I can't think of a good enough reason to do this, and I've heard just about all of them. That money is so much more valuable to you where it is, tax deferred, with the years left to compound interest or earn dividends and accumulate growth before your retirement. You should find every other possible means of retiring that debt, even including bankruptcy, if the rest of your situation warrants that. Leave your retirement funds alone. You'll never regret it.

If you've looked at all the strategies we've talked about in Chapter 6, "Your Transition Budget," and you've looked at all the potential short-term income possibilities, and it's pretty obvious that something's going to have to give, then I will suggest that your unsecured creditors will wait. They will try to make your life hell, charge you late fees, and tattle on you to the credit-reporting agencies, but they will wait. They have done it before and they will do it again. They certainly don't see it this way, but I would propose that they own some part of the responsibility for selling you a credit contract that they would have known you couldn't afford in the event of a lay-off.

Your secured creditors won't wait. They will come get the security you pledged to back the loan. So your dealings with them will need to be a little more skillful. All the way through this book, I have encouraged you to match the term of the solution with the term of the problem. The strategies that I'm going to share with you are not intended to be life-long skills that you use to maneuver your way in and out of credit contracts that you can't afford. These are strategies that will give you some sense of control in the short run and provide you the time to return to full-time employment.

MY BEST ADVICE

Don't pay off any debts while you're unemployed. If you're tempted, put the money in a savings account and celebrate the first day of your new job by paying them off then.

Dealing with Existing Indebtedness

I'm going to assume that you've always paid on time in the past. We'll start at the beginning. The first thing you need to do is turn to Appendix 9.2 and fill out the chart to become aware of whom you owe. Fill in the total amount you owe each creditor, the date and amount of the minimum payment each month, and the late fee that they will charge you if you're late. You need to research whether you have an interest rate that will change if you are late on a number of payments. You also need to look to see what your limit is on that credit account because, as late fees and additional interest are added, you may exceed your credit limit. Then you'll also incur an overlimit fee.

Once you've compared the various costs of being late on your different accounts, it may become obvious to you which one or ones are the most important to keep current. You should call the companies and ask the customer service people to review your account with you and explain these different features. It won't send up any red flags or cause the deadbeat police to show up at your house. This is information you're entitled to understand and they're happy to share with you.

Some things come out of the blue that you can't predict; like the time that Congress got mad about the student-loan default rate and slapped a 25 percent penalty on all overdue balances. (That was a fun day at my office.) You can usually, however, predict the cost that you will incur when you dishonor the contract, as long as the contract is still in force. The creditor may choose to cancel the contract, at which point you might incur fees associated with collection activity or legal filings, but you will also see, at that point, that your interest and late charges will stop.

One of the scariest words in our vocabulary is *collections.* Collection agents use it all the time to intimidate debtors into paying their bills, "If we don't get $150 by Friday, we will have to send this out to collections." If you've never been sent out to collections before, it sounds pretty scary. What this means is that they will be writing off your account on their books, taking the tax loss, and hiring a third-party collection agency to come after you. The interest stops, the past due balance goes away, your credit report shows that the balance has been charged off, and you start over again with a new company.

Collectors who call to remind you to make your payments have one of the world's worst jobs. Imagine what their days must be like: talking to people who are cranky, avoiding them, lying most of the time, and really upset that they called. I'm not suggesting that you feel sorry for them, except that if you stop to think about it, they probably need the money more than you do or they wouldn't have accepted that job. What I am suggesting is that you understand whom it is you're talking to, so that you can be effective in your communications.

Remember when you were a teenager waiting for the phone to ring? Imagine how many times the phone actually rings at a collection agency. They might leave 10,000 messages and they'll get 3 calls. If you're one of those three calls, you're going to make somebody's day. You're going to catch them so totally off guard that they won't have time to be mean to you.

Here's what you're going to say:

> Hello, my name is Pat PaidUp. My account number with you is 1234567. And I have a payment to send you on the twentieth of this month for $10. Could you mark your records for me, please?

Their response will be:

> I'm sorry that's not enough. We will need $110 by the fifteenth.

Your response will be:

> Hello, my name is Pat PaidUp. My account number with you is 1234567. I have a payment of $10 to send you on the twentieth. Could you mark your records for me, please?

Their response will be:

> I'm sorry, but we'll need to send this to *collections* if we don't get $110 by the fifteenth.

And your response will be:

> Hello, my name is Pat PaidUp. ...

Sounds like the Geneva Convention, doesn't it? Their computers have spots for your name, your account number, and the date and amount of your next promised payment. Once that information gets entered, they won't be bugging you again today. If you're tired of the collector calls and you get them to put it into their system that you have called, you will not cycle back onto their call list for at least 24 hours. Even though it isn't technically illegal to call you again within the 24 hours, most systems are designed to prevent the possibility that you will claim harassment.

Whether or not their threats are real is immaterial at this point. If you've created a budget and a cash flow based on what you know needs to get done right now in order to return to full employment, while keeping your family safe, then nothing that they say should change your mind. It's their job to push buttons and send you off balance so that you will do things that you ordinarily wouldn't do.

We've all heard that when you're under hypnosis you won't take actions that are outside your set of values. For some reason, when you're under the spell of a collector, you will. "Don't you love your children?" asked in just the right tone of voice, at a vulnerable moment, might cause you to pick up the phone and call your mother and ask her for money. That's what the collector wants you to do. But this is not the time that your mother wants to talk to you. You're upset, she'll feel coerced, and it won't really solve the problem.

Back to those people with really hard jobs. Their roles are scripted, just like any touring Broadway show you would pay $75 to see when you're working. They have a role to play. In many cases, their director (the boss) is pacing behind them, pointing to parts of the screen or a chart and coaching them to be more forceful and demanding. But at the end of their day they go back to being totally normal people with totally normal problems. They pick up their kids at day care and go back home, just like you do when you're working.

When you sit through that Broadway show and you cry, you leave thinking it was a wonderful show. The actors did a marvelous job. When you hang up the phone from a collector call and you cry, put yourself in the same place. The actor just did a marvelous job! He moved you. He changed your frame of mind. He caused you to think differently about your situation and search for new solutions to an old problem. Even if a solution occurs to you while you're upset, let some time pass before you take action on it. Talk it over with others you trust and evaluate it against the plan you have in place. Don't let an underpaid actor, whose life is more stressful than yours, rewrite your entire strategy.

Let's talk a little more about what your creditors can really do to you and when they can do it. Logic tells us that if they had any real power, they wouldn't have to be so nasty. Actually, they can charge you late fees, possibly raise your interest rate, and maybe sock you with overlimit fees when those fees add up to more than your contractual limit.

We already know that they can close your account and refer it to a collection agency. When they send it to a collection agency, they actually have fewer rights, because the debt is now covered by the Fair Debt Collection Practices Act, which regulates third-party collectors. This is a law that protects you from unreasonable harassment and interactions by the collectors. It's a fairly hard law to enforce by individuals. But if you feel you are being harassed, or other actions have been taken outside of the bounds of normal decency, you can certainly file a complaint with the Federal Trade Commission. They will use your information, along with others, to look for patterns of abuse of the law.

You also have the right to refuse to do business with the third-party collector and insist on doing business with the original creditor. You must submit this request in writing. You also have the right to request original documentation that details the amount that the collector is collecting. These strategies are not going to get you out of paying the debt but it might calm things down temporarily, while you look for work.

Another thing a creditor can do is take collateral that you've pledged against the loan. You probably have 30 to 60 days before you will hear serious threats of repossession from a creditor. Effective, positive communication could probably defer that date somewhat, but you do need to take these threats seriously. If the collateral is repossessed, the creditor will send it to a liquidator, such as an auction house. Usually the market will pay about 50¢ on the dollar for repossessed assets. You will still be liable for the difference, plus the repossession expenses. You will be left with an unsecured loan and no asset.

Finally, they can sue you. Now, technically, in our country anyone can sue anyone. It doesn't mean that they will win. What the word "sue" really means is that the creditor is asking a local court to make it official that you owe the debt and to give them more options to collect from you. It could take two to three months from the time they threaten to file to the time there is actually a judgment recorded by the court. Some courts offer alternate dispute resolution services, such as mediation, which can speed up the process.

Having a judgment will add a few screwdrivers to their toolbox of ways to get money out of you. The first thing they'll be able to do is to garnish your wages. But you haven't got any wages! Yet. Before you celebrate this fact they can, in many situations, garnish your unemployment check. It's a little harder to do but, theoretically, it can happen. Many states have an exemption amount, which makes sure you can take home most of those earnings. Some states don't allow garnishments at all, and others have wage-protection programs that enable you to pay to the court the amount that would be garnished by one creditor and spread it around to all your creditors. Some states also offer participation in a credit-counseling program to prevent garnishment. You need to learn, very quickly, how your state handles these issues. Your local courts that handle the garnishment orders may have this information or credit-counseling agencies may be able to outline the local customs. Attorneys and your local legal aid office can also help you.

These additional actions also take some time and effort on the part of the creditor. With the judgment taking two to three months, and the garnishment taking another one to two months, you've got about four months until you would see money disappear. If they have a judgment and you return to work full time, then certainly they can also attach those wages. But you may have an option of paying that garnishment directly so that your new employer doesn't learn of your financial challenges. It might be discrimination to fire you because your wages are garnished. But it certainly doesn't feel good, as a new employee, to put your employer that close to understanding the turmoil you've experienced.

With a judgment, a creditor can also seize other assets, even if the loan was not collateralized. They usually will try to locate and seize bank accounts first. If you have paid any recent payments with your current bank account, then they have your number and they know where you bank. You could see your entire balance, in any accounts you have, disappear overnight. A prudent strategy would be to not leave your money where they could get to it. However, you may be asked, under oath, where your money is and you would be obligated to tell them. If you don't have a bank account or you have the ability to cash your money out and not leave it there overnight, then this risk is not a concern. Remember that judgments are only issued against the actual creditor, and, therefore, collections on that judgment are only pursued against the actual creditor. If you and your spouse have separate accounts or separate assets, his or her money will not be affected by a judgment against you unless you commingle it in various accounts.

If you have assets or income that can be seized, and a creditor has secured a judgment against you, you may consider using the protection afforded by the bankruptcy court. The bankruptcy laws in our country protect three things:

- Your assets
- Your income
- Your sanity

It's my opinion that 99 percent of the bankruptcy filings are to protect the third. Normally, assets and income can be protected using negotiation, mediation, and subversion. But your sanity is a little more fragile and a little harder to hide. At some point, you may find yourself thinking that you just can't take it any more, and you're probably right.

A bankruptcy will cost you money because it's not advisable to file it without an attorney. The laws are complicated, and are getting more so all the time with the recent changes in our bankruptcy law. A Chapter 13 filing will preserve most of your assets, buy you time to repay your debts, and possibly write off a portion of your debt. A Chapter 7 filing will liquidate your assets and your liabilities and let you start over fresh. Most attorneys seem to prefer to file a Chapter 7. It's easier, quicker, and a little more profitable for them. The Chapter 13 takes more effort and more commitment on your part.

Back to our earlier principle, I would call a Chapter 13 filing a temporary solution to solve a temporary problem. Whereas a Chapter 7 is a permanent solution to solve a permanent problem. And the consequences of the two follow from their respective temporary and permanent natures. For instance, you might repay your Chapter 13 within three years, and a year later might be able to enter into a mortgage. A Chapter 7 will remain on your record for up to 10 years and might cause you to lose a promotion because of a questionable credit history.

An analogy, which may help you understand this, is to compare it to the treatment you might get after your foot was crushed in an auto accident. The Chapter 13 would be like the surgery, physical therapy, and crutches that you use for two years while you regain full control and use of your foot. The Chapter 7 is an amputation. Make sure to fully discuss both options with your attorney and to make sure you select the one that's right for you. Remember that attorneys do not meet with you after you have filed bankruptcy. Their job is done!

It's financial counselors, such as myself, who see the long-term consequences, both financially and psychologically, that impact people who have chosen the Chapter 7 option. If you need a long-term solution, it works wonderfully. It can be filed very quickly, it's relatively inexpensive, and it relieves the pressure almost immediately. The same could be said for the amputation. But you will be left with new problems to deal with that may not be fully explained at your attorney's office.

Credit Counseling

It will be helpful for you to know how credit counseling works and what to expect when you get there. Credit-counseling agencies are springing up all over the country in different forms. The old-fashioned brick-and-mortar agencies exist in most metropolitan areas and in many smaller towns. There are also several online credit-counseling agencies, most of whom were originally brick-and-mortar companies, or mergers of several of those firms.

Most credit-counseling agencies are nonprofit corporations, which means they don't have stockholders and they don't pay taxes on their income. They were formed by and are sponsored by the credit industry. The oldest one was formed by a department store in my hometown to help customers who had fallen behind on their charge-account payments. They wanted to keep these folks as good customers but not embarrass them about their bills. They opened an office a few blocks down the street and hung out a sign to encourage those individuals to come in and work out a reasonable payment plan.

The concept was successful, and today thousands of these offices exist. They are still funded by the creditors. When you sign up for a debt-repayment plan at most agencies, you will have no, or a very small, monthly fee to process these payments. The bulk of their expenses will be paid by the creditor when they withhold a percentage, usually 15 percent, from the payment that they send on to your creditor. Let's do the math. If you pay your credit card $100 through a credit-counseling agency, the credit-counseling agency receives a fee of $15, and your credit card company gets $85. On your credit card statement, however, it will show that they have received $100. Because of this tight relationship, the credit-counseling agencies are often able to negotiate lower payments, lower interest, suspension of late fees, and other terms that are favorable to you.

A counselor will go over your entire budget with you and identify those obligations where that sort of modification can be made. Then they will rebalance your budget against those new payments. If you are receiving unemployment compensation as your only source of income, chances are you will hear, "You don't make enough money." You already knew that. They have fairly strict guidelines that they must work within, because in the last few years, the creditors have become stricter with them as their success rates have fallen and their competition has increased. Some large creditors have stopped doing business with them, believing they can get more out of you if they try to collect directly.

Many credit-counseling agencies have very caring and competent counselors working for them who will try to help you develop a strategy that you could then work on your own if you don't qualify for their debt-retirement program. But the reality at most agencies is that you have one hour to meet with your counselor and then they're booked solid for the next two weeks. They have a very high demand and diminishing income. The future of that industry is even more uncertain given the high demands that this new bankruptcy bill might place on them.

My encouragement would be to seek out an agency that appears to have skilled counselors who could spend the time with you that you might need, but don't be disappointed if it isn't a magic pill. They can only do so much; the rest will be up to you. If you qualify for their debt-retirement program, it will be reflected on your credit report, and many future creditors will look at it as any other third-party intervention, such as a Chapter 13. The credit counselors may have relationships with local creditors to enable you to reestablish credit or get a car loan, and so on, after you're out of their program. But I wouldn't rely on this to rebuild your credit report in the future.

MY BEST ADVICE

Develop your plan and keep the creditors in perspective. Don't let their collection strategies refocus your attention from securing employment and keeping your family housed, fed, and safe.

Avoiding New Indebtedness

There are all kinds of ways to get into debt: The obvious ones, such as living off your credit cards, and the not-so-obvious ones, like deferring the taxes on your unemployment check or the withdrawal you took from your 401(k) plan. Many people rely on their family members to help them out during a period of unemployment, and that's one of the reasons to keep families strong. I'm sure you've helped out others when they've hit some bumps in the road, and it's nice for them to return the favor.

There are different ways to structure family loans and assistance that can preserve the family for better times ahead. Some people will just come out and ask, "What can I do to help?" The first answer to that question is to ask them to pay for or purchase for you the items that are specific to your job search, things that are not part of your normal budget and are a direct result of your current layoff. This keeps them out of your normal budget decisions and also helps them feel as though they really are helping to turn this situation around. It's a win-win.

I always advise family members who loan money to other family members to deliver it as a gift with the following message, "This is a gift. If someday you choose to repay me with a gift, I will accept it." So if you are offered a gift, it's important that you accept it with the message that you will accept it and hope that someday they might accept a gift from you. This keeps you both adults and both loving adults in this transaction. Any money that changes hands with any other message than that between family members creates a parent-child relationship between the two adults. This is not the time in your life when you need to feel like a child. You need to be up and out of the house every morning, acting as the most mature adult that you can be.

If no one is offering help, it might be because they don't know how. If you know that there are members of your family or friends who would want to help you if they knew your real situation, you can certainly tell them. Make sure that you've thought through the consequences of not receiving help from them and that you're sure you couldn't handle it on your own. Many times, people are more than happy to help out with extra child care or other needs of your children while you're job searching. Structure your requests for help in a way that will make them feel valuable and needed. Chances are that they're very worried about you and they want to know what will make a difference.

Given your lower income, you may not currently qualify for new credit accounts, but you may own accounts that you haven't used or that haven't reached their limit. It will be very tempting to use these accounts to continue your lifestyle without making any reductions in your budget. Remember that the only collateral on this debt will be your future earnings. Since those earnings are in question, you really have no idea how much debt repayment you can afford. These may end up being the worst debts that you have, because if you reach the point of needing to declare bankruptcy, they may be disallowed because of their newness.

On a high-interest credit card, if you borrow $2,000 and repay it at the minimum repayment amount, you will end up paying back over $7,000. So if you find yourself needing to use unsecured credit to pay for ongoing expenses, put a price tag on that item of four times what it says on the store shelf and ask yourself, "Is it worth that to me?"

Good reasons to use your unsecured credit cards are few but they do exist. For instance, if your solution to your situation is to sell your home, and you need to do some touch-up or fix-up to it to make it more marketable, using your credit card to finance these improvements would be justified. At the sale of your home you can retire that debt along with your mortgage. A student loan to enhance your skills or make you more marketable, which can be deferred until you're employed, makes a lot of sense. As you make decisions to use unsecured debt, keep in mind the rule of thumb that the only *good* debt will enhance the value of an asset or increase your income. When you find yourself financing day-to-day expenses, it's time to rethink your strategies. Next to cashing in your 401(k) plan, this will be the most expensive way to bridge the gap.

I'm very aware that this is all much more easily said than done. And I have personally witnessed the turmoil of thousands of families as they faced traumas equal to or greater than a layoff. My true mission is to have you end up better off than you started. Be careful of strategies in which you are deferring the pain to a later date. You want to get through this, put it behind you, and move on as a stronger financial individual. Adding to your unsecured debt will not accomplish that goal.

MY BEST ADVICE

Avoid the hair of the dog. New debt is not the solution to old debt. It may feel better for a time but the financial hangover will last much longer.

What You Should Know by Now

1. Whether you need to see your credit report right now or you can wait.

2. How to get your three credit reports when you need them.

3. Where you are going to save any money that you will use to pay off debts when you are reemployed.

4. What your current debt portfolio looks like.

5. What fees and consequences there will be for paying late on each debt.

6. Which debts you can let slide if you have to.

7. How you will communicate with your creditors.

8. How you will avoid incurring new debt while unemployed.

Next Steps

1. _____

2. _____

3. _____

4. _____

5. _____

6. _____

7. _____

8. _____

10

Housing and Mortgages

Have you ever stopped to think what business your mortgage company is really in? Lending money, of course! The business they are *not in* is real estate. And they don't want to own yours! It does them no good to take your house from you. It is a major hassle for them and often causes them to lose lots of money in the process.

Whenever someone loses his or her job, a universal panic follows: "What if I lose my home?" Stop right there. You are not going to lose your house. You may choose to sell your house, or move to a different house or city. But with the least bit of planning and communication, your house will not be taken from you.

Now that we have that out of the way, you are ready to learn some decision-making strategies that will help you through the often-difficult options ahead.

The Feasibility of Keeping Your Home

Quick! How much does your house cost you each month? If you just quoted me your mortgage payment, you are so wrong. And you know it, but it's not easy to think about all the other costs when you don't have any income.

You're going to hate this, but if you are really serious about wanting to make sure to hold on to your house, you have got to do it. Appendix 10.1 has a chart to fill out to help you determine the exact cost of owning your home. Some things are pretty straightforward, and others you will want to argue about.

We could get in a prolonged battle over the real, true, undeniable cost of maintenance. Real estate professionals have calculated that we (as in everyone in the country) spend 3 percent of the value of our homes *every year* to keep their market values. That means that you build your house again every 33⅓ years, sort of. Think about it: If you walk into a home that hasn't had a new kitchen in 25 years, you notice, and you wouldn't pay as much for that house. So not everyone spends this 3 percent, but their homes' values reflect that fact when they go to sell them.

Appraisers call this deferred maintenance. I bet you are deferring as much maintenance as you can right now. You are living with things that would have driven you crazy a few months ago. But they can wait, can't they? So if I were to ask you to show me your budget, it would have a really low number next to the home maintenance line right now. You are either in denial that anything will ever break again in your home, convinced that you just fixed absolutely everything right before you were laid off, or more realistically, you are ready to live with broken stuff.

Now that you know that I know that you are not really spending 3 percent of your home's value in repairs this year, just write it on that line. No more arguing. Trust me, we are looking at the big picture here and trying to make one of the biggest decisions you will make in the next few months. Let's do it right.

After you look up or estimate each of the items and do the math, I want you to look at the cost of renting a comparable dwelling. This will bring you closer to understanding the true cost of homeownership. I am not specifically suggesting that you consider renting, but the analysis will be helpful. It will give you a sense of what your options are and whether you should fight harder to keep your home.

This analysis might also help you to understand why you have accumulated home equity line or credit card balances. You may have been living in a home that was really unaffordable all along. In that case, your layoff was only a wake-up call. It didn't cause the problem. Many homebuyers *qualify* for mortgages that they really can't afford. They find it more difficult to make other adjustments in their lifestyle after they buy their home than they anticipated.

The chances are that you will learn that, in the long run, you can afford your home and that in the short run, the cash-flow shortage is all that you need to fix. It's important to know this before you go to bat. If the numbers tell us that you are going to need to find less expensive housing, it's better to not go through months of struggle, just to end up moving anyway.

MY BEST ADVICE

Your housing is your most expensive budget item. Take the time to really figure out how much it costs you. Don't fight to keep it if you couldn't afford it to begin with.

Will Refinancing Help?

When your grandparents were ready to buy their home, they put on their Sunday best and drove downtown to the savings and loan association where their families had always done business. They sat down with Mr. (it always was a mister) Banker and nervously applied for their mortgage. Then, for 30 years, through thick and thin, they made their mortgage payments at the same office. Quaint, huh?

Fast-forward 50 years, you watch slick advertisements, apply online, negotiate over the phone, shop around, and have your payment drafted out of your money-market account. You also make your payment to a new mortgage servicer every other year or so. You have no personal connection to anyone whom you would feel comfortable telling that you feel like you've just been sucker-punched. I bet the last thing you want to do is pick up the phone and tell a 20-something customer-care representative that you might be defaulting on your loan in the near future. No, not my idea of an exciting afternoon, either.

You know where I'm going with this one, don't you? Yeah, you need to call them. Not right now, but soon. Talking really does help. They get these calls every day and they know what to do to help. Remember the most important thing: They don't want your house!

Obviously, they would love it if you could just keep making those payments as scheduled. But they would also enjoy knowing, in advance, if you can't make them in full or on time. If you have already missed a payment, call them immediately, before they call you. In many companies, the "client counselors" are different people than the "collectors." The counselors are not the ones calling you. Need I say more?

So what can they really do? They can choose to allow you to miss a payment or two, and make it up over several months after you are working. Be careful of this option, unless you have really worked your budget to know that you can make that extra one third of a monthly payment. The worst situation you can find yourself in is needing to default on a special payment arrangement. It just doesn't sit well. Don't make promises you can't keep. The customer-care folks won't be quite as nice the next time you call.

They can also offer you a line of credit, second mortgage, or a refinancing of your first mortgage. They could even create a first mortgage that is amortized (spread out) in such a way that you are paying a much lower payment for a while and then a larger payment later.

The second most important thing to them (next to not ending up owning your home) is keeping you as a customer. You may not feel like an Olympic-class customer right now, but they know you will be back on top in no time, and you will remember their willingness to work with you.

My earlier cautions about using debt to finance your expenses during a layoff are slightly amended when it comes to your mortgage. Extending the term of your mortgage or financing payments with a second mortgage are probably justified, if you have determined that your home was affordable to begin with and your new working budget will be able to handle the payments. Be careful about asking for cash-out, however. Go back to the previous chapter if you have forgotten, already, why this is a dangerous option.

You may be wondering how a person with no or little income qualifies for a mortgage. Well, you're certainly not going to be buying your first home when you're unemployed, but refinancing an existing home is usually pretty straightforward. Depending upon your history with your mortgage company, they may not even ask for income and asset verification. You will want to look at your credit report before you apply for any refinancing, to make sure there aren't any errors or blemishes that will need to be explained. You are not in a mood to have to do that, I'm sure.

If you find yourself with a bruised credit history, and especially a history of late payments with your mortgage company, things get a little trickier. Again, this may be a signal that you were holding onto a home that you really could not afford that was causing you financial stress. You may need to seek refinancing from what is gently referred to as the *alternate solutions* market. You've seen their ads, too. They provide a wonderful service for families who need financing, but can't meet the qualifications of the mainline companies. Be more careful than ever about shopping around and inquiring about fees before you apply. You will probably ask for interest rates and assume that the closing costs are normal, but they can be two to three times the market rate. So ask.

Usually, you can refinance back to a competitive market rate after 18 to 24 months of good payment history. So this qualifies as one of our short-term solutions to a short-term problem.

MY BEST ADVICE

Remember that refinancing is not free. Even if you don't have to write anybody a check, the fees are added to the loan and you will pay them someday, with interest. Shop around and be the best consumer you know how to be.

How Far Can You Push the Mortgage Company?

As hard as I have tried to convince you that nothing bad is going to happen, the reality is that your mortgage company is like a lion. They can sleep wherever they want to. If you find that your mortgage company is acting like a lion that was just woken up when he didn't want to be, then other measures are in order. You have several options.

Obviously, you can sell the home. In many markets there are real estate brokers who specialize in investment properties. They may be able to locate a buyer who could buy your home and lease it back to you. It's worth a couple of phone calls.

Many social-service agencies and credit-counseling agencies around the country have qualified housing counselors. In addition, they may manage local programs designed to prevent foreclosure actions. The Department of Housing and Urban Development (HUD) runs The Housing Counseling Clearinghouse (HCC), which can help you find a counseling office in your area at their automated information line, 1-800-569-4287.

I would recommend meeting with a housing counselor before calling your attorney, as their services are free to you. If things have heated up to the point that action will need to be taken before you can get an appointment, then an attorney can also help you. They can negotiate with your mortgage company on your behalf or use the bankruptcy code to help you keep your home.

If you start talking early to your mortgage company, and keep talking as your situation evolves, you shouldn't have to push them at all. But, generally, even though your note probably says that you are in default when your payment is 30 days late, they won't begin foreclosure action until 60 to 90 days. This is still not a lot of time to develop a good plan. Start working on it as soon as you know you have a problem.

MY BEST ADVICE

Take every communication from your mortgage company and local courts very seriously. Open your mail immediately and pick up any certified letters quickly. Keep copies of everything you send and receive from them. Document all phone calls. Stay in touch as frequently as you need to meet your needs.

Do You Live in the Wrong Place?

Your home is more than four walls and a roof. I know that. An old adage advises, "Don't love anything that can't love you back." Your house may not technically be able to love you, but it keeps you close to those who do. Your neighborhood, school, church, grocery store, parks, and so on, all bring you feelings of acceptance and love. Your house keeps you near all those things.

There are certainly other homes in the general vicinity of your home, unless you're bucking for the sequel of *Northern Exposure* to be filmed at your place. You might be able to find another, less-expensive home or apartment in your area.

If you're having trouble finding work, you may need to leave the area. Before you make this decision, it would be helpful to look at some labor statistics to find out if it is time to jump ship. The U.S. Department of Labor and your state's Unemployment Compensation department will have pounds of data on how jobs are faring in your city. It is possible that, as bad as it is, you are in an area doing better than other counties in your state.

You may also learn that you are at the end of a downward cycle and that things are looking up, even though you haven't felt it directly yet. The Department of Commerce collects a variety of data. *Leading Economic Indicators* that try to predict the future movement of the economy are published each month in the Business Conditions Digest available at www.doc.gov or at your local library. Some of the indicators that you may be interested in are as follows:

- Average workweek for manufacturing
- New orders for consumer goods and materials
- New orders for plant and equipment
- Changes in inventories

- Number of new businesses started
- Building permits for new homes

These are called leading indicators because they change first. Then, the economy expands or contracts as a result, creating or eliminating jobs.

By looking at this data, some of which is available by industry, you can locate an area that might be more promising. It is hard to know whether to move before you have a job. Sometimes job searches are difficult long distance, even though the Internet has made us all virtually next door.

If you have been seriously considering beginning your own business, which we will talk about in more detail in Chapter 15, "Business Opportunities," you may want to stay where labor is available. Depending upon what you will be selling and to whom, you may want to move to an area with higher employment, so consumers have money to spend at your business.

Another issue that comes up frequently is the split family. One wage earner moves to secure employment while the other parent remains with the children to finish a school year or wait until the house sells. This is always challenging and expensive. It takes a lot of work to get resettled after this type of upheaval. Give it the attention and time it deserves and stay focused on the long-term benefits.

MY BEST ADVICE

People move all the time, but that doesn't make it easy. If you decide to move, focus on the positive and look forward to the new life you are about to create for yourself and your family.

What You Should Know by Now

1. How long you will be able to make your mortgage payment in full and on time.

2. What the true cost of owning and maintaining your home is. What the comparable cost of renting is.

3. What options your mortgage company is prepared to offer you if you lose your ability to pay on time before you return to work.

4. What the latest communication from your mortgage company said.

5. What your credit reports show, if you are going to ask to refinance your mortgage.

6. Where a local housing counseling agency is, if you should need to talk with them.

7. The name of an attorney who works with real estate and bankruptcy law, should you need his or her services.

8. The specific economic conditions of your county and whether or not they are improving.

Next Steps

1. _____

2. _____

3. _____

4. _____

5. _____

6. _____

7. _____

8. _____

11

Savings and Investments

We could have a fun debate over the concept of an *emergency fund*. How I define it is not as important as how you've defined it in your financial planning process. Is an emergency an unforeseen event or is it an event that requires quick action? You may have thought of your emergency fund as your "rainy day" money, your "just in case" money, or your "mad" money.

Many people think of their emergency fund as the place to go when the car breaks, the refrigerator dies, or the kids' feet grow all at the same time. All of those items are not really emergencies, by the first definition. They are not unforeseen events. Cars break, refrigerators don't last forever, and kids need shoes. That's just reality. But they were all events that needed quick action.

Your current period of lower income is the reverse. It was an unforeseen event, but it may not require quick action on your part in the same way that a car repair would. If you've been following the standard financial planning guidelines and have three to six months of your income in a relatively liquid investment, then your decisions in the coming weeks and months are going to be relatively calm. Combined with your unemployment insurance, a reduced spending level, and some good investment choices, your savings may last well beyond the three to six months.

If you have between three to six months of your income saved, but the money isn't liquid or you haven't paid the income taxes on it yet, then your decisions will be a little more complicated. You will still survive an extended layoff with little financial upheaval. You will probably begin immediately to rebuild your emergency fund.

If you haven't accumulated the recommended three to six months of income and you have told yourself that you can rely on available credit sources as an emergency fund, then this period of lower income will probably become very stressful. You may be subscribing to the theory that your credit will be available for ready cash until you can liquidate some longer-term investments. This, again, will obviously require more strategic planning and thought over the next few months.

If you were thinking that the credit sources by themselves would be a source of available cash, you'll find out eventually that a period of unemployment is not the time to be incurring new debt. My guess is that once you're back at work, you will quickly change this attitude and make sure that you begin building an emergency fund for the next time that your income drops.

The rest of the chapter is for those of you who have accumulated even a small amount of savings outside of your retirement plan and IRA accounts. You'll want to maximize the use of those funds during your period of unemployment and help to guarantee the most security for your family.

MY BEST ADVICE

Once you are back at work, build an emergency fund exclusively for unforeseen events. Do not use the money for predictable events that may require quick action. Choose investments that are liquid and not tax deferred, such as money market accounts.

Update Your Balance Sheet

Your balance sheet is a piece of paper or a computer file that lists everything you own and everything you owe. I've always thought that it was kind of funny that we call it a balance sheet, because the last thing in the world we want is for it to balance. We'd really rather that it be lopsided. We'd like to own a lot more than we owe.

The reason it's called a balance sheet is that back before the dinosaurs, accountants put another little section on it called "net worth." Your net worth is the difference between what you own and what you owe. When you add your net worth to the smaller of the two, it equals the larger of the two, and, therefore, it balances. If you have to add money to what you own to equal what you owe, then your net worth is negative. If you have to add money to what you owe to equal what you own, then your net worth is positive. This is a good thing.

In Chapter 9, "Credit Issues," you listed all of your current debt obligations, so half of your work to complete your current balance sheet has already been done. Now we need to look at the other side of the sheet—your assets. An asset is something that you own that someone else would pay you money for. It could also be something that you own that makes you money, whether it has any value to someone else or not.

There is another distinction that some people make. They refer to some assets as "use" assets. These are things that you use and happen to have value that someone would pay you money for, such as your car or your tools or your computer. Appendix 11.1 gives you some ideas to think about the types of things that you own that might be convertible to cash should you need the money. There are five different values that each of your assets has:

- What you actually paid
- Actual cash value
- Depreciated value
- Replacement value
- Ability to generate income

The first one is what you actually paid for it. Many times this is the most unrealistic value to place on the item, but other times it's the only value you've got. For instance, you may have purchased your home a few years ago and you haven't had it appraised since then. Its original value may be as accurate a number as you've got for this purpose.

You might be able to find out what other homes in your area have recently sold for. This second way of valuing assets would be the actual cash value of your home right now. Its value may have gone up since you bought it or it may have gone down. Other assets, such as cars, normally will go down from the date that you purchased them. So the actual cash value is the amount that someone else would pay today for that specific asset.

The third valuation is what accountants might call the depreciated value. Assume that you bought a computer for a home business. Your tax preparer may have helped you to decide how many years you would take to depreciate, or deduct, that expense on your tax return. If you are depreciating it over three years, its value would be two thirds of the purchase price after one year, and one third after two years. After three years, that item has no value in the IRS's eyes.

The fourth way to value an item is the way that you may think about some of your assets for insurance purposes. This is called the replacement value—how much you would need to spend to replace that item today. This is the value that many people assign to their assets in error.

The fifth way to value an asset is by its ability to generate income. You might own a piece of rental property that makes you $500 per month after expenses. In order to generate that same $500 a month from an investment, you would need to have $120,000 invested at 5 percent. So to value your asset as an income producer, its value might be $120,000.

Depending upon your purpose for this information, your balance sheet might end up looking very different. Our purpose right now is to capture the actual cash values of each of these assets in case you need to convert them into cash. We also want to, in our chart, look to see which of these assets are currently generating income and how long we predict it would take to change each asset into cash. Those three pieces of information will be very important as you make decisions in the coming months for you to maintain your cash flow.

MY BEST ADVICE

Everything you own, you inherited or you bought for a reason. Each item will have emotional strings attached to it. There are some things that "it would kill you" to have to sell. List these items with zero value, because in order to find a market price there has to be a willing seller and a willing buyer. You are not a willing seller in this case.

You May Need to Readjust Your Goals

Every item on your balance sheet got there somehow. You inherited it, received it in a divorce settlement, got it as a gift, bought it, found it, or stole it. It either came from someone you love or someone you now hate. It could have been a good decision or a bad decision. It has done well over the years or it's caused you nothing but grief. Whatever it is, there is a story behind it. And, even more importantly, there are some emotions that accompany it. You're really proud that you got into that stock when it was only two dollars. You really don't like the manner in which that company's voicemail treats you when you call. Or you wish you'd never bought that thing because it's brought you nothing but trouble.

I have spent a good amount of energy in this book trying to convince you to examine and honor your emotions. It would be counterproductive for me to try to talk you out of honoring the emotional side of your investments. With your heightened adrenaline levels and difficult decisions ahead, you can't help but make some of these decisions in a less-than-rational frame of mind.

I would like you to identify the piece of each of your assets that is filled with emotions. Maybe there's a stock that your mother left to you when she died. Maybe there's a gift that you received from someone dear to you. And maybe there's an account at your ex-husband's favorite bank and you'd really rather not do business with them anymore. I'd love you to make the perfect, purely financial decision that will lead you toward the optimum level of financial security for your family. But I know that righting some of these wrongs or holding on through hard times to a gift that someone gave you can bring a tremendous sense of control and success. Appendix 11.2 will help you decide the emotional value of your assets.

I'm going to bet that this temporary period of unemployment will not be the end of the world. But it may be the temporary interruption of one or more financial goals that you have set for yourself. If you have a college-bound child and you know how much you would like to have in their college fund by the time they apply, you might not be able to do that at the same pace. This may mean that the child will need to supplement the funds you accumulate, or the child may need to wait a year to enter school, or the child may need to use student loans to finance his or her education. It doesn't mean that the child won't go to college.

You may also need to adjust your retirement plan. You may find yourself needing to increase your contributions to your 401(k) at your next employer, to defer your retirement date, or to reduce the amount of retirement income that you expect to enjoy. It doesn't mean that you won't retire.

In the short run, this may mean canceling a vacation or putting off a home improvement. Practice readjusting your goals instead of canceling them. Instead of hearing yourself say, "We won't be able to take the trip for Katie's graduation," you might hear yourself say, "We'll need to take the trip for Katie's graduation next year."

Just as feeling pain in your feet after suffering a spinal cord injury is a good thing, so is feeling pain of not being able to reach your savings goals after a period of unemployment. You've set the goals and they are important to you. The pain you are feeling is a sign of financial wellness. It tells me that you have a strong underlying respect for the power of savings in your life, and I know that will not change. Once your income is back at its normal level, you will be right back saving and reaching goals as you have in the past. Just because your plan needs to be changed doesn't mean that it wasn't a good plan.

MY BEST ADVICE

Realize that the best plans are those that can absorb change and continue to produce good results. Use your current situation as an opportunity to learn how to develop financial plans that can absorb interruptions.

Investments That Match Your Transition

Let's go back to Appendix 11.1 and ask several questions:

1. Is the investment generating any interest or dividend income?

2. Is the investment worth less or more than when I bought it?

3. What would the taxes be if I sold it?

Most investments that you own as a working individual are not set up to send you monthly income. The types of investments— mutual funds, individual stocks, and bonds that send you checks in the mail—are the types that many retirees rely on to supplement their pensions. At this point in your financial life, you have probably opted for investments that reinvest their earnings. They may have no paid-out earnings and instead are growing in value. You will enjoy this growth when you cash them out someday.

A simple switch to throw might be to ask your mutual-fund company or stockbroker to have your investments send you the income instead of reinvesting it. In a mutual fund, you're paying income tax on that money in this tax year, anyway. You might as well use it to supplement your income.

If you find yourself needing to cash out investments while you're unemployed, it might be a very good time to sell items that have large capital gains. If you are in the middle of a tax year where your income is much lower than normal, you might be able to take the capital gain, pay the tax at a much lower income bracket, and have a hidden benefit by doing so. If you're near the end of a tax year in which you've had fairly normal income, you may want to wait until January to cash out that specific item. You may want to use money from investments that have a loss first, so that the loss can help you with your tax liability during the current tax year.

Many times, when we're short on cash we look at the tax consequences of a financial decision as being not important because we can deal with it later. The tax-filing date always comes quicker than we think it will. Postponing the effects of a taxable decision can just spread out the pain from your current situation.

If your cash position is not strong at the beginning of your period of unemployment, you may want to make some adjustments in your assets as soon as possible to allow for the calm transition of funds into your budget as needed. The investments that would match your transition period would be cash equivalents or very highly rated bond or blue-chip stock funds with very low volatility. You will not have months or years to wait out a dip in the stock price if you need the cash from that investment now. Even if an investment appears to be at a six-month's historical low, it's not a good strategy to wait two or three months until you need it, because the chances are it could be even lower. You may feel firsthand the reason that financial planners have recommended the three to six months in an emergency fund held in cash or cash equivalents. Cash does not fluctuate, even though it erodes with inflation, and its value will be very predictable over your unemployment period.

MY BEST ADVICE

Look for ways to adjust your investment portfolio that will provide you the most security while minimizing the tax liability.

How Long Will Your Money Last?

Your transition budget from Chapter 6, "Your Transition Budget," will give you your strongest clue to this question. If you have increased your supplemental income and adjusted expenses as much as you can, the difference between the two will be your budget shortfall. The assets that you have identified as an emergency fund are those that are desirable for you to liquidate. Possibly you had that very purpose in mind for them when you initially bought them or they have no other use or emotional attachment for you. Add them up and the calculation is simple. Divide that amount of money by your budget shortfall to get the number of months that it will last. Appendix 11.3 will walk you through this calculation.

You have other assets on your balance sheet that you are not counting as part of your emergency fund, and you now know how long you have until you need to start making a decision about liquidating them. Some of them might take a good amount of time to liquidate, such as a house. If it appears as though your emergency cash will last for seven months and you know that selling your home might take you three months, then at the four-month mark you need to make the decision to sell your home.

This can sound pretty grim, but I would recommend thinking about it in the following manner. You don't have to think about selling your home for four whole months. In fact, you shouldn't think about selling your home until the end of four months. This enables you to refocus your energy on securing new income without thinking about an option that is totally undesirable.

Things will become more difficult once you see yourself needing to liquidate items that are of use to you or have an emotional attachment for you. Let's take the fishing boat that he buys or the above-ground swimming pool that she buys. I can't recall how many times I've heard, "And I can always sell it if I need to." So many times we justify purchases by their presumed value in the future as part of our emergency fund. But, when it really comes down to it, we don't want to get rid of them. And they might not really have as much of a value on the ready market as we thought they would.

MY BEST ADVICE

The time spent worrying about having to sell assets that you would rather keep is time you should be spending securing employment. Identify the date in the future when you will have to begin to make those decisions and forget about them for now.

What You Should Know by Now

1. How much of an emergency fund you have accumulated.

2. How much of your emergency fund was actually available credit on open revolving accounts.

3. What assets you might be able to convert to cash, if needed.

4. How soon you will need to begin to prepare those assets for sale.

5. Which investments can be altered or positioned to generate more current cash flow for you.

6. Which investments would be advantageous to sell from an income-tax perspective and during which tax year.

7. Which assets you would rather not convert to cash for emotional reasons.

8. How long your money will last.

Next Steps

1. _____

2. _____

3. _____

4. _____

5. _____

6. _____

7. _____

8. _____

12

Hiatus Activities

You've got a break. With some hard work and a little luck, it will be a short break. Use it to your advantage to refocus your thoughts and energies into directions that will benefit you. Creativity will be the key because you won't have lots of extra money to spend on these activities. Staying busy and exploring new things are tremendously positive ways to keep a clear mental focus and a high sense of self-worth.

Personal Development

You can divide yourself into three parts: a body, a mind, and a spirit. Personal development is a process that takes all three aspects of your being and helps them to integrate together while building your overall capacity as a human being. Developing one while ignoring the other two does very little good. Let's start with your body. You might think it's not a very pretty subject. But if being a star on *Baywatch* is not on your list of possible careers moves, don't sweat it. Let's instead think about what you can do next to develop your personal health and well-being. Think about it this way: on a scale of 1 to 10, if 1 is the worst shape you've ever been in, and 10 is the most toned, active, healthy person that you know, where are you right now? Are you a one? Is this it—the worst shape you've ever been in? Or have you begun moving up this ladder already?

Whatever number you picked, I want you to add one to it and then answer this question: If I had said that new number instead of the original number, what would be different right now? Think about what would be changed in your body for you to answer the next number up. Maybe there's a pair of jeans that you would be able to fit into, or a set of stairs that you could run up without getting winded, or a stretch you could do without cheating. Just work toward that. Maybe a walk around the block each evening after dinner, or a couple of minutes of stretching as you get out of bed each morning, might be all you need to begin that sense that you are moving in the right direction. It certainly won't hurt.

You might also turn your attention toward your diet and look for subtle ways to begin improving your daily nutrition. In this, and in all other areas of your personal development, I'd like to encourage you not to make major overhauls at this exact moment. Your focus needs to continue to be on your job search and your next career move. Diverting your attention to big projects that involve major changes in your lifestyle might be a way of avoiding the reality of your job search. Use small steps that bring you a sense of satisfaction and move you toward new levels of personal development without allowing them to take over your day.

The second area of personal development is your mind. Look for ways to expand your world and create new ways of thinking about things, again without undertaking overwhelming projects. Follow more closely a political issue that's always interested you, search the Internet for information on an interest you put aside years ago, read the book you got for your birthday last year, or send e-mails to friends you haven't seen in years. Keep your brain active with challenging and interesting dialog.

If you're spending your days around children more than you used to, look for opportunities to surround yourself with adults. Attend discussion groups at your local library or church. Volunteer your time at an agency that promotes adult literacy or helps the homeless.

The third aspect that needs development is your spiritual life. Religious organizations throughout the world have organized to provide people with structured paths toward spiritual growth. During a period of unemployment, people who have chosen one of these paths in their lives usually find it to be a tremendous source of strength, comfort, and encouragement. It is also a time when many people return to or seek out that structure for their spiritual development.

Connecting with others less fortunate than you through volunteer service work is also a very powerful way to enhance your spiritual growth. Most churches and social service agencies will easily guide you to activities that will require a specific time commitment and tasks that are easily accomplished. Many communities have central hotlines where individuals willing to offer their time and talents can call to find out about the needs in their community.

For most people, volunteer work provides a much bigger impact to their feelings of self-worth than paid work could ever do. Whether it's an hour each month, or 20 hours a week, a volunteer assignment can keep you grounded in values that are important to you, activities that connect you with other caring human beings, and tasks that remind you of your competency as a worker.

The added benefit of this type of activity is that people who are engaged in multiple responsibilities within their family and community suffer less depression when they're not employed. If you're already involved in volunteer work in your community, you know this instinctively. But, your immediate reaction upon losing your job may be that you can't afford the time to spend in those activities when you need to be looking for a job. This couldn't be further from the truth. You lost your job, not the rest of your life, and it needs to continue exactly as before in order for you to remain strong and ready for your next assignment. Use Appendix 12.1 to help you think of ways to develop these three areas.

MY BEST ADVICE

Put aside some time each day for yourself. Choose an activity that contributes to your physical, mental, or spiritual health. Your strength in these areas will be obvious to prospective employers and give you an advantage in a competitive job market.

Professional Development/Retraining

If your job was eliminated because your entire industry is going away or your employer was using outdated technology that no one else recognizes as a valuable skill, then you may find yourself in a position where you will need to step up your skills before a new employer would be attracted to you. A lot of these skills, however, especially computer skills, could be mastered in a week or two by getting a good manual and sitting down and practicing them.

Even if an employer you're interviewing with has on-the-job training, it's not a bad idea to go ahead and get a jump start on those skills. Most prospective employers are extremely impressed if, between the first and second interview, you've already read the manual. This shows a tremendous interest in performing well for their organization. You may, however, have the attitude that reading the manual for a job that you don't even have yet is a supreme waste of time. That attitude will surely come through in interviews and prevent you from obtaining jobs that you feel you are qualified to do.

When we get beyond computer skills, things get a little trickier. For instance, you may lack a level of certification or a particular licensure that many employers are looking for in your field. You know you have the skills and the capacity to do those jobs, but you just don't have the right piece of paper. You may want to think about how you secured the last job without that piece of paper and whether there are other employers who similarly overlook that detail. Maybe you were working for the last employer on the planet that allowed a person without the credential to do the job that you were doing. If so, you probably knew that it was only a matter of time before you were going to be required to step up your credentials. If you are committed to your field and it's really what you love to do, then hurry up and get it done. Any amount of time that you delay will be time that you're working outside of your chosen field, probably for less money than you are worth.

Moving up to the next level of your profession, however, is a very different proposition. Let's say that you have a Bachelor's degree in business and you've always wanted an MBA. Beginning an MBA right now could do one of two things. It could excite you, put you in a position of seeing new and better opportunities for yourself, and create a flow of thoughts and dialogs that makes you very interesting to future employers.

It could also do the opposite. It could divert your attention from the necessary job search and drain your energy from appearing employable to your next boss. I would examine the question of whether you were about to begin a period of additional schooling had you not been laid off. If you are ready to handle both the pressures of work and school at the same time, then you may be mentally prepared to do it now.

Remember, though, that starting school and planning to tackle a new job at the same time creates a tremendous amount of pressure. And, given the fact that many employers do provide at least partial tuition reimbursement, it might be better to secure your next position and then return to school once you're firmly established in that position.

The last area to consider is changing careers entirely. This is something that takes time and patience and a plan to achieve. It's normally better accomplished by moving voluntarily from your last place of employment into your new career. Having just involuntarily been separated from your last employer may not be the best time to totally start over. Your income may be lower to begin with and it may be a while before you can qualify for a position in that field if you need to return to school first. I would recommend returning to a position in your previous field while you establish the savings, get the training, and look at your options for changing careers. Again, if this is something you have been planning, and the timing of your layoff makes it reasonable to go ahead and do it now, then I wish you a wonderful transition.

Another area of professional development, which is a little different than skill training, is the area of work behaviors. Every work environment has a different set of expectations placed on its workers. This set of behavior norms is called "culture" and every workplace has one. You will fit into some cultures and you won't fit into others. You've probably been doing a lot of thinking about how you interacted with your previous work environment. You know what you liked and what you didn't like. You know which personalities you enjoyed and which ones drove you crazy. You know which bosses you felt like going the extra mile for and which ones you hid from. You know which people you wanted on your team when a project was due and which ones you would find other problems to divert them to. An important part of your professional development as you look for work is to determine who you are and what kind of environment you work the best in. Are you the kind of person who is hurt when your co-workers don't remember your birthday or someone who cringes when they do? Do you find the morning management meetings a time to learn how your co-workers are handling their pressures or are they a total waste of time? Are you more comfortable in an environment where high achievers are given awards and have their names up on the wall or where they are ridiculed by their co-workers for being show-offs?

You did all this work the last time you changed residences. You knew what size of yard, type of garage, and kitchen layout you preferred. You went looking for it. Spend some time to learn who you are and what type of environment you're most comfortable in. Then go look for it. Check out Appendix 12.2 to discover your fit with different corporate cultures.

MY BEST ADVICE

School takes a lot of energy away from a job search. If you were already in school or about to start, go ahead. Otherwise, wait until you see what the demands of your next job will be.

Projects, Hobbies, and Travel

In your transition budget, you may find yourself cutting out most of the extra activities that you enjoyed while working. As we talked about how to downsize your budget, I suggested that you keep as many of the activities as you can, but find ways to do them for less. For instance, you may have enjoyed going to professional sporting events, which can be very expensive. During your hiatus period you might choose to go see college or high-school events that provide you the same interaction with the sport, but will cost less than half of the money.

Most people who enjoy hobbies have an accumulated reserve of supplies and projects that they haven't completed. You might even find this a good time to go ahead and work on many of those backlogged projects and sell them at a bazaar or craft show for a little extra money. They can also make very nice birthday and holiday gifts during a time when money is tight. Most hobbies bring people an outlet for creativity and a sense of control that is very calming, especially in a period of crisis.

Some projects cost nothing and are a lot of fun. Try going through old pictures and labeling the backs. Some hobbies cost very little, like beginning to research your family tree or learning to square dance. Other hobbies have very expensive costs associated with getting started, such as playing a musical instrument, or photography. Think cheap and fun. Don't put added pressure on your financial situation by getting into something that is hard to maintain without a lot of money.

Look for a common interest with other family members as a way to increase the amount of positive time that you spend with each other. Developing your skills at a card or board game costs nothing and gives you a lot of opportunity for fun times together.

Traveling is a hard thing to budget when your income is low. But sometimes getting away is very helpful to you and your mental health. You may not get much vacation time for a while at your new job, either. Group trips sponsored by churches or other organizations, visiting family members you haven't seen in a while, and camping are all ways to get away while spending less money. Many times, service organizations need people to travel to areas of natural disasters. This may not sound like a vacation but it certainly is something that you wouldn't have the opportunity to do when you're working full time. Your skills would be very important to the effort, and the experience is usually very rewarding. List your fun activities in Appendix 12.3.

MY BEST ADVICE

Find an activity that is fun, relaxing, and cheap. Use it to stay close to people you care about and take your mind off your job search once or twice a week.

New Relationships

When you start your new job soon, you will be forming lots of new relationships. This is something that you may not have had to do in a long time. And one of the things that you can use your time between jobs to do is to practice this process. We've covered a lot of situations in this chapter where you might be putting yourself in brand new situations with a lot of new people. It might be a class, a church group, a bridge club, a volunteer organization, or a community project. There will be people there, and many of them you won't have known before.

Use these opportunities to watch yourself and see how you interact with new groups of people. Do you wait for them to approach you? Do you make a conscious effort to remember their names? Do you immediately start to psychoanalyze them? Do you look for a way to take a leadership role? Do you decide right away whom you don't like? Which of your patterns are helping you to integrate with the group and feel comfortable as a member of that group, and which of them are distancing you from the group or causing you to feel uncomfortable?

Make it a game to find one interesting thing out about each person in the group, and focus on that interesting thing as something that can be the basis for your relationship with that person. Your relationship will grow when they learn that you're interested in them. They'll enjoy sharing with you that aspect of their lives that you find interesting. Many of these relationships will be transitional or short-lived and, therefore, are very low risk.

Use your time in these situations to practice the approaches that you will use as you enter your new workplace. Those relationships will be long-term and therefore more invested. The way you begin them will set the tone for a long and productive membership in that group.

MY BEST ADVICE

Meet as many new people as you can in situations where you have a chance to get to know them. You will benefit from the new relationships as people who can help you network and stay connected to groups of adults while you are out of the workplace.

What You Should Know by Now

1. What you will be doing to enhance your physical well-being.

2. What you will be doing to develop your mind.

3. How you will continue your spiritual growth.

4. If you will need to step up one or more workplace skills.

5. If you will need to enroll in a formal course of study.

6. What type of work environment you will feel comfortable in.

7. What hobbies you can engage in that are fun and cheap.

8. How you can continue to meet new groups of people.

Next Steps

1. _____

2. _____

3. _____

4. _____

5. _____

6. _____

7. _____

8. _____

13

Finding the Next Job

In my earliest days in the financial planning world, I was trained to be a life insurance salesperson. There were lots of strategies, skills, and systems out there to make me a top producer. But, what it really boiled down to was numbers. The people who had been around the block a few times would say that I had to place 100 phone calls to get 10 appointments to make one sale. Lovely.

That wasn't all: They went on to tell me that I should be happy, no, *ecstatic*, when someone says "No!" Because, you see, that's one step closer to the *one* who will say "Yes!" Get it? If you've been in sales at sometime during your career, you get it. If you haven't, it sounds like a snow job. Being happy about rejection is a little like being warm in Minnesota in January. You have to work at it.

We've all heard the "never hurts to ask" philosophy. All they can say is "No." Right? But who wants to hear 99 nos? Or worse, hear nothing, and imagine that the answer will be no when it finally arrives? Patience is a hard thing to muster when time seems to be standing still.

How to Use Your Outplacement Services

Guess who isn't going to find you a job? The term "outplacement" is a bit of a misnomer. They aren't really going to *place* you *out* there somewhere in that big world of business. Some firms now prefer "Career Transition" or "Career Management" to the term "outplacement."

These distinctions are, of course, a lot more important to them than they are to you. What you care about is where your next paycheck is going to come from and when. Your employer hired them to get you going toward that goal. They will let you vent, encourage you, teach you skills, strip you of some self-defeating attitudes, and give you a game plan. They are the coach, the cheerleaders, the team-trainers, and the fans, all rolled up into one. But you are the one who still has to play the game.

Depending upon your employer's contract, you may interact with their counselors and trainers from one day to a year or more. During that time they will teach you how to update your resumé, network, search for openings, create job opportunities that didn't previously exist, and sell yourself during an interview.

Years ago, outplacement was only offered to highly compensated individuals and was very personalized. As it has filtered down to the rest of us, it has become more generalized. Group counseling and training are used more often these days to deliver motivation and information. In the past, they would work with you for as long as it took for you to get a job. Now they contract for time-limited services.

Most outplacement services are offered by a handful of large, national companies. Every large city also has boutique firms that are smaller and may have more customized services. You won't be in a position to complain to your employer that you would rather be working with a different firm, but you may be able to switch counselors within a firm. If you are not clicking with the person to whom you were assigned, tell them. If they aren't effective, it costs the outplacement firm money. They want you to have someone you trust.

Outplacement services are like an all-you-can-eat salad bar. My advice is to literally stuff yourself so full that you can't walk. Take every topping they've got. If you ever hear that little voice in your head say, "I don't need …," do it anyway. If your ego needs an excuse, how about this: The others in the group will benefit from your already having solved that problem. Just do it. You'll never know what great ideas you'll get until you do.

What if you are in the 20 percent of laid-off workers who do not get outplacement services purchased on their behalf? First, complain to your employer. They may not be aware of how helpful it can be and how important it is to you.

If that doesn't work, ask them if they would be willing to help you with some of your needs. While rewriting your resumé, you could ask to show it to your HR department. They see them all the time and could give you a grade on it. Your previous manager, co-workers, and subordinates would be a great source of insight into which strengths and skills you should highlight on your resumé.

Your HR staff might be willing to let you practice interviewing. They do this all day long, too, and might be able to give you some pointers.

MY BEST ADVICE

Use your outplacement services for what they are intended. Use them as much as you can, but don't expect them to find you a job.

Other Services You May Need

If you have been planning your exit from this company and just happened to get laid off before you got to the door, you may have already researched some of your options. But if this was a total surprise, my guess is that you will be a little confused. The outplacement counselors will have opinions about what works and what doesn't. And they won't be afraid to share them with you.

You are probably a good consumer. You check around, compare prices and quality, and then make decisions based upon your needs. The problem is that you are in crisis right now, and a lot of those standard operation procedures may be thrown out the window. Scoundrels know that you may not ask all the same questions when you're desperate. Remember that.

If you can't or don't like to write, get help with your resumé. Write it first in your own words, as bad as they are. Say what you want to say. Use a book or other guide to get you started. Then, find an editor. Don't ask that person to write it. That resumé has to be consistent with what you would say about yourself in an interview. You will be the one answering questions about it. The editor may rearrange it, shorten it, fix it grammatically, and make it pretty. But they shouldn't write it. You do that.

If you hate to interview and sell yourself, you need practice. Career counselors and job coaches are great resources for enhancing this skill. If you can't afford them, ask your minister, friends, family, and previous manager if you can practice with them. Sometimes it's the stage fright that we need to work through. Repetition helps.

Some of the most valuable experiences in a job-seeking process are free. Support groups are forming everywhere. Churches, Internet sites, and networking clubs are in every community. In the end, it will be a *person* who makes the decision to hire you, not a company. Interacting with as many people as you can find will continue to improve your ability to sell yourself and your confidence to do so.

Another service available to you is an employment agency. There are two basic kinds, distinguished by how they are paid. Search firms (unwillingly called headhunters) are paid a retainer to find you. They are paid, by the way, whether they fill that job or not. You can shoot your resumé off to them, if you like. If they happen to have a job that fits you, you'll be included in that search process. But they don't work for you and won't respond to you as if they do. Many job postings on the large Internet sites are posted by search firms. You may end up talking with them as you identify positions you are interested in.

The other type of firm is paid on contingency. A commission is calculated against your annual salary when they match you with the job. They may have a standing contract with a large employer, receive individual openings as they occur, or try to place you in advertised jobs. These firms work with all types of positions and employees. Occasionally an employer will post a job that they are not willing to pay the commission for. The firm may offer you that job and tell you that you would need to pay the commission. There should be a job somewhere for you that you don't have to pay to get, but if the offer is perfect and you don't want to wait any longer, you could decide to pay the fee.

One measurement of quality in these firms is their treatment of your credentials (resumé). Can you have the right to approve where your resumé is sent? If not, you may want to find another firm. If you have been interviewing with ABC Company and then your employment agency sends them your resumé, you have just cost them that commission to hire you.

MY BEST ADVICE

Be smart. You are the customer. Act like one. Ask questions. If it sounds too good to be true, you'll know that it is. Trust your instincts.

This Is a Job

So what kind of a job is it, anyway, where you don't get paid but you have to keep working? I can think of lots of them, some very rewarding. Parenting, volunteer activities, and political activism come to mind immediately. What do these all have in common with your job search? You believe in them and the outcomes matter to you.

So if your job search is feeling like drudgery, it's simple. You don't believe enough in yourself. You haven't found the economic activity that you feel you are worthy of doing. This is the number one requirement to convince your next employer to believe in you enough to hire you.

Certainly you have to sell to your market, but the secret is that most jobs are created to fit the person sitting there. If you have enough confidence and can communicate that to a potential manager, that manager will find a place for you in her department. She needs creative, energetic, flexible people to meet her goals.

Your insight and experience may just get her to readjust her goals. She may see a new solution to an old problem sitting right in front of her. You're hired!

So this job you're doing right now has a purpose: to identify the activity that brings you the highest sense of self-worth. If you could define the perfect job, what would it be? Are your skills there to support that job? Can you see yourself doing it? When you can, then go figure out who needs you.

So many times, job searches are conducted upside down. We read the ads, which represent about 10 percent of the jobs available. Then we conclude that we have to fit into one of those positions. We turn ourselves into Silly-Putty trying to look like a person who would fit into that job. Nobody wants to hire Silly-Putty.

But they do want to hire you. If you know who you are, that is. Figure it out and do it soon. Use a self-assessment tool, hire a counselor to help you, or do it on your own. This work should really be done before you write your resumé, because your resumé should reflect what you've learned about yourself.

Once that work is done, the rest of the job is just going through the motions enough times that you achieve success. You will try to be efficient and maximize your efforts while minimizing the time it takes to secure employment. But even inefficient job seekers get hired. You don't have to be the best kid on the block at this. Job-seeking is not your life-long dream. Your career is.

Each day you will go to work at the job of finding a job. You will have a schedule, a routine, and a set of goals. But you will also respond to interruptions, inquiries, and requests for information. It's sounding a lot like work, isn't it? If you focus on the outcome, you will be productive. Appendix 13.1 will help you schedule your job-hunting tasks.

If you sit back and believe that a job will come to you, all you will get is lazy. It's a campaign, it's a mission, and it's too important to let anyone else take control. If you're still processing your anger, use it to your benefit. Channel that energy into positive actions that will help locate that next employer.

MY BEST ADVICE

Be your own boss. Have a daily strategy session with yourself. See if you are doing your job of finding a job.

Looking Outside the Box

You don't have to look outside the box. You *are* outside the box! You want to get back in it, right? Back to that predictable, safe world of regular employment.

So what's going on out there? You haven't been out there for a while and things are a little different, I bet. Whatever culture we cling to has us believing that the rest of the world works just about the way we do. Not!

Now is your opportunity to upgrade your cultural software. The business culture that you were captured by wasn't doing as well as it could have been. You might still be there if it were.

But you were "voted off the island"! You get to experience the rest of the world for a while, before you go back and eat rats. Do they really eat rats on the other islands? Maybe not.

While you were maintaining your position at your previous employer, you were being given positive feedback that you were doing a good job. Am I right? But you were doing things that ultimately were proven inefficient or unprofitable by the marketplace.

Now is a good time to look at what part you played in your layoff.

- Were you eager to absorb the positive reviews and yearly raises, knowing deep down that you weren't really contributing to the bottom line?

- Was your department ever really respected in the corporate organizational chart, but you stayed there anyway?

- Did you continue working on a particular product line well past the point of profitability?

Maybe the problem was just a jerk or two. All companies have them, you know. They have to work somewhere, and we haven't passed a law yet saying they all have to work together. Wouldn't that serve 'em right! What was it that they did that drove you nuts? Who did they remind you of from the fourth-grade playground?

Looking outside the box means looking in places that don't take you back to the same old situation—an unproductive department with a jerk running it. But amazing as it sounds, that's probably what you're looking for. You may not like it, but you know it, and that is much easier than learning something brand new.

Knowing and honoring who you are includes knowing the kind of environment where you shine.

- Do you need independence and clearly defined outcomes?

- Do you need daily assurance and others to keep you going?

- Does competition or cooperation keep you motivated?

- Is a team-oriented or hierarchical management style more your preference?

Once you define where you will shine, it doesn't mean that you will be able to find exactly the situation where you will not have to adjust anything. Inflexibility is one of the most commonly sited reasons for including someone on a layoff list—and seeing them remain unemployed for a longer than average time. You may be asked to change your attitude about any number of things, including pay structure, working conditions, location, or seniority.

Along with defining where you will shine, you need to define those aspects of a job that are critical to you. Make sure the list isn't too long, or you will be waiting a long time to find a job.

Then, match those criteria to the list of jobs you have been considering. Are they consistent? Let's say that your number one criteria is staying in your community, but you have been looking for jobs in your industry—and the last employer in that business in your community just laid you off. You're either going to be changing communities, changing industries, or enduring a long commute. Refer to Appendix 13.2 to help you determine aspects of the work environment that are important to you.

At some point you will begin to feel that this is a crisis you have control over. Many things that can happen to us are totally out of our hands. This one is right in your palms. Once you realize that you are already outside the box, looking there shouldn't be so scary. It's an opportunity, an adventure. These are rare moments when you get to peek inside other boxes and see what makes them run. Use that information to your advantage.

MY BEST ADVICE

It's normal for people to seek out situations that they know. But you've already made the break from a less-than-optimal situation. Don't go back.

What You Should Know by Now

1. How to best use the outplacement services offered to you.

2. How to substitute other services if you haven't been offered a comprehensive package of outplacement services.

3. What activities bring you a sense of self-worth.

4. How you will communicate your highest productivity to a potential employer.

5. How you will structure your workday as a job-seeking individual.

6. How you will set goals to absorb rejection as part of the overall process.

7. What type of work environment will enable you to do your best.

8. What job features are the most critical to you.

Next Steps

1. _____

2. _____

3. _____

4. _____

5. _____

6. _____

7. _____

8. _____

14

Evaluating Job Offers

As job offers begin to come in, and they will, you have the new task of evaluating their appropriateness for your situation. The value that you receive from your employment is not just limited to cash you can deposit in your bank account. It includes non-cash benefits, deferred income, and many intangible benefits that are very important to you. The process of evaluating them can be rather complicated.

At first, the prospect of just working again, anywhere, might sound wonderful. And the comments that you might hear from critical relatives, when they've learned that you've turned down an offer, might be more than you could imagine enduring.

When an employer is ready to make you an offer, they have already gone through a very specific process during which they evaluated your skills, your attitude, your experience, and your references. They have eliminated or placed you ahead of other job applicants for that position based on some criteria that they set prior to beginning their search for qualified applicants.

It's important that you give yourself some time when receiving a job offer to reflect on its value and possibly submit a counter-offer. You should have a similar set of expectations and a process for evaluating the offer that you receive. The best opportunity that you have to change the terms of your employment with your prospective employer is before you accept the job. They have already determined that you are acceptable under their conditions. Now it's your turn to determine if their offer is acceptable to you. When they communicate the offer to you, ask for a face-to-face meeting within two to three days to have all of your questions answered.

How Much Is Enough?

There's really only one answer to how much you should ask for from your next employer—what the market will bear. If you've been working at the same company for a period of time, at least long enough to get a couple of raises, your last payrate may be out of step with the market. Your company's internal policy regarding pay increases may have had nothing to do with the market for replacing your skills. It may have had more to do with a traditional plan of pay increases that was started years ago and is not market driven. Many workers who stay at companies for a long period of time know that they are making more in that job than they would out on the market because their company's pay raises have bumped their pay up above market levels.

If you are working in a job that was paying you more than the market wage, you likely created a lifestyle based on that income. You entered into debt and other ongoing obligations that required that level of income. You will now have three options:

- The first is to increase your skills up to the income level that you've become accustomed to.

- The second is to decrease your living expenses down to the income that the market will offer you.

- And the third is to work more hours at the lower level of pay so that your overall level of income remains stable.

The opposite can also be true. Employees may be enticed to stay at a company for less than market wages because other working conditions are favorable to them. They may receive other benefits as a result of having worked there a long time that they wouldn't be able to replace with another employer immediately.

Just because you were making one amount of money at your last job doesn't mean you aren't worth 20 percent more than that to your next employer. What you need to do is the same sort of analysis that that real estate appraiser did when looking at the value of your home last time you refinanced. One step in that process is to look at what they call comparables, or "comps" for short. They look at homes in your area that are similar in size and features that have sold recently. And they look at what the market paid for those houses. You would want to do the same thing regarding your own marketability. Look at people who have similar backgrounds and education to yours, who have recently been employed in the market where you're seeking employment. See what wage they were able to command for their services.

A second thing a real estate appraiser does is look to see if your home has any special characteristics that might increase or decrease its value to a potential buyer. You can do the same. Are there specific skills or experiences that you have that most of the other people seeking the same sort of employment don't have? Or are there specific things that you're lacking?

Another thing that appraisers will look at is how many homes are currently available on the market and how many people are seeking homes of that type. We call this a buyer's or seller's market. When more employers are looking for people like you than there are people like you to be found, you would be in a seller's market. You would be able to increase your price based on the higher demand compared to supply. If the opposite is true, and there are a lot of you and not very many employers needing your services, then it will be a buyer's market. Wages will be forced down because of the competition.

For you to say, "I made $58,000 in my last position and would like to make at least $60,000 in my next one," has no bearing on reality, because it isn't market-based. The market may say you're only worth $55,000, or the market may say you're actually worth $65,000. In the first case, you'll waste a lot of time looking for a $60,000 job that doesn't exist. And in the second case, you'll lose $5,000 a year by taking a job at lower than what you could command.

Employers know that most unemployed workers are willing to take jobs at or near their last salary level. That's why they ask what you made. They don't want to offer you more than they have to. They also want to know if they have any chance at all of attracting you to their company, based on the knowledge that you won't go too much below your last salary level.

MY BEST ADVICE

Markets change constantly. Don't sell yourself short or hold out too long for a salary that doesn't exist in your market.

Evaluating Benefits

I'm not really sure any more what defines great benefits. It used to be that a company could add the newest bell or whistle to their benefits package and claim that they had a progressive benefits program. As the cost of those benefits continued to rise, they began asking their employees to "share" in that cost. The joke here was that the employees had been paying them all along by accepting lower cash wages for their productivity. By lowering their gross pay to help pay the cost of these benefits, the employers made it more official that wages needed to be lowered as benefits increased.

Many benefits became nothing more than a group purchasing contract where there was a possibility that the employee might get somewhat of a discount on that service or product over what they would have paid on the street. Benefits departments began looking for more and more services that cost them nothing other than a little bit of administrative paperwork. Things such as free checking at a bank where you signed up for direct deposit, or free delivery of groceries, were added to the list of employee benefits.

I know that this type of benefit is convenient and nice to have. However, it adds very little value to an analysis of the actual compensation that you are being offered from a prospective employer. There is a big difference between an employer saying to you, "We have long-term disability benefits" and an employer saying to you, "We pay for your long-term disability benefits." If you don't qualify for disability insurance because of your health history, then either of these statements would represent a great value to you. But if you are insurable, just having a policy that you can purchase from them does you no good and, in fact, may harm you if the cost for that policy is more than what you could buy on the open market if they didn't offer you this benefit.

The best way to evaluate benefits is to look at the employer's contribution to the cost of that benefit. This is money that would be in your paycheck if we didn't have this custom of group purchasing in place. Health insurance, of course, is the most costly benefit that employers are offering around the country. It is probably the most critical to you in terms of evaluating a job offer.

Many times you will be shown, or you will ask to see, how much it costs you to insure your family under their plans and what types of plans they have available. This is one way to look at a benefit they're offering you, but I would suggest that you look at it from the other direction. Instead of asking how much it will cost you, ask what the total cost of the coverage is to the company and how much the employer is contributing to that cost. That is your true benefit. Because you saw the COBRA cost, as you exited your last employer, you should be able to calculate what your previous employer was contributing to your health insurance premium. Subtract what used to be deducted from your paycheck from the COBRA cost. That was your benefit at your previous employer.

If you have done what I suggested in Chapter 7, "Insurance Decisions," and shopped for various health-insurance options for your family while you were unemployed, you have a very keen awareness of what it will cost in your area for your family to be insured. It's possible that the coverage that your prospective employer is offering you is actually more expensive than what you would pay as an individual for coverage that you value. If their contribution to that cost is not enough, then you haven't actually received any benefit by joining their plan.

If they offer a cafeteria-type plan where you can use benefit dollars in some other area, you might be better off to keep your individual policy and allow those dollars to be spent on some other type of coverage, such as disability insurance.

When you evaluate retirement-plan benefits, come at it from the same direction: Don't be concerned with the proportion of money that you can contribute to the plan. Be more interested in the amount that they plan to contribute. If there's a Defined Benefit plan, ask what a normal contribution that someone in your income range would receive each year, and with a Defined Contribution plan, ask what percentage of your income the employer contributes. Many times, this is based on your contribution, or what's called a matching contribution; for purposes of comparison, you should use the maximum match that they will be able to do for your income level.

Another benefit that you will need to evaluate is the time that they offer you that you don't have to work during each calendar year. This could include sick days, vacation days, personal days, professional development days, and anything else that they've thought of to call days that you don't have to show up at work. Unless you're planning to work a second job during some or all of those days, their value to you is in raising the average wage that you earn during the days that you are working.

A quick example would be this: Let's say you were earning $36,000 a year or $3,000 a month on the average, but you had four weeks of time that you didn't have to work and you were still paid. What this really means is that you earned your $36,000 in 11 months, not 12, and you earned a little under $3,300 a month on the average, or an annual rate of $39,000.

This is a technique you can use to compare jobs that are offering you different amounts of vacation time. Most people who are used to standard employment contracts get very upset when they have to take a day off with no pay. They have come to expect to be paid whether they're at work or not. Employers figured this out a while ago and have just adjusted their compensation schedules to pay you less per week and hold back the money you would have earned for the days when you want to stay home. It's a hidden savings account that the workers in this country have asked their employers to manage for them. You may have built up a lot in your hidden savings account that was just handed over to you at your layoff, if you received a lump sum check for your vacation pay.

Some jobs allow you to bank those days and work them instead of taking them as time off. If you are a person who doesn't take all the days allowed, that adds to your overall income from that employer over time.

Another piece of the benefit picture, which is important to evaluate, is how long you have to work with that employer to qualify for the different benefits that are offered. You can look at the one-time cost of this by calculating how much it will be to continue those benefits on your own until they kick in with your new employer.

Another one-time cost would be that of relocating. Many employers will pay relocation allowances and help you with selling your home and other associated problems with moving. These are a lot harder to quantify in a quick analysis because many of the variables aren't known. What you can do, however, is to ask the same sort of questions. How much would they be contributing? And if you're comparing two different offers, those numbers can be analyzed.

Sometimes on the list of benefits, at various companies, will be an item, which might be called Profit Sharing, Bonus, Incentive Pay, or anything that implies it's going to be calculated on something other than your time at work. The professionals who design compensation systems around the country have tried lots of different strategies for getting employees to believe that they make more money than they do. One of the things that many employees seem to like is wage deferrals.

You would think that if I offered you a particular wage and then said, "But I'm going to hold back 10 percent and give it to you at the end of the year," that you wouldn't like that very much. But for some reason, most workers love it because they're never told that that was income they earned last January. They think they need to wait until December to get it. And, at that point, it's a bonus, it pays for their holiday gifts, and they're happy. Their neighbor, who's been making 10 percent more than them all year, but who didn't have that money held back and given to them in December, is unhappy.

Beats me. Especially since the company has the option to not give you that 10 percent in December and not have you claim that they've unfairly withheld your wages. Even though employees will say they can't count on that wage deferral, many end up doing exactly that and structuring their budgets around an expectation of those additional earnings.

MY BEST ADVICE

Reduce each and every item on the list of benefits to the cash value that the employer is contributing for that benefit. Add that to their offer of cash to determine your total compensation offer. Compare it to the same analysis of your last job and any other offers you have received.

Comparing New Income to Old

It's important that you go through a thorough analysis of exactly what the change will be in your new income that you've been offered. Appendix 14.1 helps you combine, in one place, all of the different factors that go into analyzing your total income. In addition to the two areas we've already discussed in this chapter, the salary offer and the benefits, there are costs associated with working that can vary greatly at different employers: for example, transportation, clothing, miscellaneous office expenses, and possible day care.

Let's take transportation, first. If you'll be using a different mode of transportation or traveling a great distance, one piece to consider is the out-of-pocket expenses to maintain a vehicle, buy fuel, or pay for transit fares. Your time spent in transit is the second piece to consider. Some value needs to be given to that unproductive time spent getting to and from work.

A second expense that needs to be analyzed is the cost of clothing and other expectations of your new workplace. Many work environments have dress codes that can be read prior to accepting employment. If the dress code of your new environment is similar to that of your old, then you'll have no change in that cost, so it needn't be listed. If, however, it's very different—maybe you'll have uniforms in your new environment where you had to wear business suits in your last environment—this will actually reduce your clothing expenses.

There's a similar issue with regard to other expected office expenses. Is this an office where people are expected to eat out together each day? Is it a workplace where birthdays, babies, and weddings are all celebrated with expensive gifts? Will you be supervising a group of workers where you will be expected to dig in to your own pocket for gifts that the workplace is used to? And will you be required to maintain a vehicle of a higher quality than you would normally choose if you were just driving back and forth to work? Some workplaces require their employees to contribute, regularly, to charities or political candidates and causes. Many times this is a very public contribution that is then withdrawn from your paycheck. You might absorb it as a cost of doing business, but it's still nice to know, before you accept the job, approximately how much that will be.

There may be other expenses of your life that change because of a specific job that you have. If you have day care expense, it may go up or down based on a particular work schedule. You may have personal-care expenses such as hair or nails, which require more attention in certain work environments than in others. And another very important consideration is whether the other wage earners in your household have their income affected by your accepting this position? Maybe they can now carpool with you and get to work an hour earlier, enabling them to earn some overtime.

MY BEST ADVICE

Just as a business looks at net income (income after expenses) to see if an activity is profitable, you should deduct work-related expenses from a job offer to see the net income you will be left with.

Comparing New Work Conditions to Old

No two work environments are exactly the same. The ones you know the best, obviously, are the ones you have personally worked in. Chances are, the next place you work will have some things in common with your old jobs, and some things will be very different. Just because they're different doesn't mean they're wrong. Especially if they're in areas that you've found difficult at your last employer.

Appendix 14.2 has a place for you to list the top five things that you would like to see the same as places you've worked before, and the top five things that you'd like to see different from the places you've worked before. As you receive job offers, you can refresh your memory as to what is important to you and see if the majority of those items are consistent. If you've been unemployed for a while, any offer reasonably close to the income that you're looking for is going to sound like a good one. But if none of your work conditions are met, you're probably going to be miserable very quickly, and wish you hadn't accepted the job.

Remember that you're looking for a situation in which your particular personality and work styles will be valued. If it's obvious to you from the beginning that this is not the case, and you choose to accept the offer anyway, be very clear as to why you are overlooking those needs that you have. You'll need to look for a way to meet those needs outside your workplace. If you're feeling pressured financially to accept an early offer that may not be appropriate for you, then look at this new job as a temporary solution to your temporary financial stress. Work very diligently to remedy those problems, putting yourself in a position to embark on another job search as soon as things are stable.

MY BEST ADVICE

Ask as many questions as you can, and talk to as many employees of the prospective employer as you can, to determine if it is a good fit in the areas that aren't part of the official offer. These are impossible to quantify but will define the quality of your next work environment.

What You Should Know by Now

1. What you are looking for in an offer of compensation.

2. How to compare and contrast various benefits packages.

3. What questions you would like to ask a prospective employer *after* they have presented an offer to you.

4. What expenses you incurred at your previous employer to maintain that employment.

5. How to analyze the change in expenses you will encounter at a new job.

6. What job conditions are important to you.

7. What job conditions you cannot tolerate.

8. How to compare the conditions of a job offered to you to your previous job.

Next Steps

1. _____

2. _____

3. _____

4. _____

5. _____

6. _____

7. _____

8. _____

15

Business Opportunities

The lion's share of the jobs in this country is created by small businesses. The hard reality, however, is that most new businesses fail within the first three years. The most prevalent reason? Money.

It takes money to make money. We all know that, but we don't truly learn that lesson until we try to start a business without it. You can have the greatest idea since control-top pantyhose, the best people, a waiting market, and abundant suppliers, but unless someone is willing to risk his or her capital, it won't work.

Many businesses get started by people, such as yourself, tired of working for *someone else*. They are convinced that their only security lies in working for the only person they can really trust, themselves.

Creating Your Own "Job"

Let's reflect for a while on what a job really is: a set of tasks performed by you for financial gain. A job can be performed by an employee, a self-employed person, or a contracted business, which, in turn, employs or subcontracts for the work to be done.

You can perform jobs directly for the consumer or for customers who take your work and package it, ship it, advertise it, and insure it on its way to the consumer. In the end, you are always working for the end consumer, but your customer may be someone buffering you from them and their uncollectable accounts.

I always chuckle (to myself) when I hear someone say that they want to work for themselves. I tried that once and found out I couldn't afford me! The reality is that we always work for others if we want to be paid money. If you choose to be an *employee,* you are really asking for your employer to provide a shield of security for you, to protect you from the consumers.

Think about all those departments that your last employer had: Marketing, Sales, Customer Service, Shipping, Design, Manufacturing, Purchases, Finance, Accounting, Investor Relations, Human Resources, and many more. You didn't need to think as much about the tasks handled by departments that you didn't work in. That wasn't your problem. You were buffered.

To be self-employed is to remove some of that security and add more flexibility. This was summed up years ago by a local "Entrepreneur of the Year" when he said, "I love working for myself. I get to work half a day. And I get to pick which 12 hours that is!" Now, that's flexibility.

This status has been defined and refined by the income tax codes in recent years. You might provide the exact same services to a corporation as a *contractor* that you did as an employee. If you only have one customer and they control how you perform your duties, they will have a hard time explaining to the IRS why you are not an employee for tax purposes. This boils down to three things. They are responsible for half of your Social Security contribution, covering you for unemployment insurance, and providing workers' compensation coverage.

They will also find themselves in trouble if they don't cover you with employee benefits that must not discriminate.

If you are working for more than one customer, and are controlling the manner in which you provide your services, then you are a *contractor* in the eyes of the IRS. You will receive a 1099, instead of a W-2, from your customers. You will file a Schedule C with your 1040 from now on and similar schedules with your state and local income tax authorities. You will file a Schedule SE to pay both halves of the Social Security contribution. You will be eligible to cover yourself with your state's worker's compensation insurance.

You will be wise to begin your self-employment with the rule of thumb that half, that's 50 percent, 50¢ on the dollar, will go to taxes. As your expenses increase, those dollars will be deductible and, therefore, not taxed. But you don't get to spend those on yourself, either. I advise all people starting out as their own boss to take each check they get from a customer and split it into two pieces. One piece goes directly into a savings account for the taxes. If you were employed, your employer would be handling this for you. Now you have to do it for yourself. If you find that you can't or won't do it, this is not the way you should structure your "job."

You will also be responsible for designing your own benefit plans. You will be able to set up tax-qualified pension accounts that are designed for self-employed individuals. You will be responsible for your own health and disability insurance. Most health-insurance contracts will cover you if you are healthy. Most disability contracts will cover you after three years of consistent income. Depending upon your income and age, these costs could be another 20 percent of your income.

Many consultants in the business world are currently charging from $1,000 to $2,500 per day. It sure sounds like a lot of money. After expenses and taxes, those rates will shake out to between $50,000 and $125,000 take-home pay, but only if they work every day. And they don't. So their net income isn't that different from when they worked as an employee. They are just much more aware of all the costs and taxes that their employer used to handle for them.

MY BEST ADVICE

In comparing the income from employment to the income from self-employment, take all the taxes and employee benefits into account that would be paid for by an employer. This can run up to 50 to 70 percent of your self-employed gross wage.

What Is the Investment Required?

Going to work as a contractor or consultant rarely requires a tremendous investment. Many times your new customer will reimburse you for out-of-pocket expenses. You would only be required to front them for a month or two. You may or may not require an office or work area to work from.

You will have to get used to budgeting for lots of things that you used to expect your employer to pay for. Conferences, education, office supplies, and phone calls may not be reimbursable. This is a shock to some who have not been used to business expenses coming out of their household budget.

The main investment is usually in marketing costs. If you don't market yourself continuously, you may find yourself right back here in a few months. Retainer clients, as they are called, are nice and usually necessary to maintain a consulting practice, but your dependence upon them will begin to feel like being an employee who can be laid off.

Let's change gears and talk about starting a small business, where you are not just providing one small piece of a company's needs as an individual. You would be selling many customers a product or service that you would develop, create, package, sell, ship, and insure. You may have a facility, staff, multiple suppliers, and a need for more capital.

The experts will say that to start this type of business you must be willing to support yourself from savings or other family income for at least six months. Heck, if you could do that, you wouldn't need a job, right?

If you have been planning for some time to begin a business, have a business plan, and have raised or saved the capital that it will require, then now might be the best time to get it going. Losing your job might have been that final kick in the rump to get you to jump in and get it done.

If losing your job caused you to think about starting a business for the first time ever, then you're not ready. Go get a job for a while, as you develop your business plan, raise your money, and test your markets. If it is a good plan, it will wait. Anything that needs to happen today will probably be outdated tomorrow. You need a plan that will grow and thrive for several years, at least.

Developing a business plan can be a very exciting activity. The research, analysis, and writing that goes into it will take you to new levels of both passion and frustration. You will learn how much you truly believe in the product and in yourself. You will also learn how much others couldn't care less. They've heard this type of scheme before.

All babies look pretty much the same: shriveled and ugly. But to their parents they are the most beautiful things on Earth. Businesses are ugly, too. They have problems, risks, conflicts, challenges, and not much chance of survival. But to their founders, they are precious. Parents will sacrifice almost anything for their children, and business owners will do the same for their businesses.

We have literally picked apart your emotional stability through-out this book. It isn't great right now. It won't be for a few weeks or months. That's really quite all right. But it doesn't make you the best candidate to begin a business. Your height-ened adrenaline and capacity for denial will skew your ability to analyze business opportunities squarely. You may not be able to get out of a business financing deal or a lease that you sign before you are ready to really make a business work.

I hope that we have agreed that if you are starting a business right now, instead of seeking employment, it is because you have been planning it for some time. If you haven't, then we are agreeing that you will continue to seek employment and begin *planning* to start a business. Agreed?

A business plan is like a crystal ball. When it is turned on, you should be able to see the future of your business activity. You will use words and numbers to detail this activity. Sample busi-ness plans are available from the Small Business Admin-istration to help you cover the areas that are important. A great place to start with any business planning need is www.sba.gov.

The two most important things you will learn from your busi-ness plan are …

1. How much money you will need to start the business.
2. When you can pay it back.

You will have a natural tendency to minimize the first and to speed up the second. People never believe that they need as much money as they will, or that it takes as long to pay it back as it will. When I was starting my first business years ago, I heard what I thought was a pretty funny joke, "Take the capital your business plan says you need, and multiply it by 10. That's what you really need." Unfortunately, it's not a joke.

MY BEST ADVICE

Don't start a business just because you are unemployed. Start a business because you have written a solid business plan with the help of advisors and know that it will have a good chance of succeeding.

Where to Get the Money

Stories are everywhere about how some wildly successful businesses were started with a crime. Fraud, theft of secrets, embezzlement, and so on, are all options. Not very good ones, though. You can imagine how people who are very passionate about their business plans might justify an illegal means to accomplish their ends. Don't do it. It rarely works for long, and it adds a layer of risk that can't really be measured.

More legitimate ways to finance businesses are around. Make no mistake, it is not easy to finance a start-up business, and you will be on the line personally in almost every choice.

First, and most simply, you can use personal money. Money that you have inherited or earned can be invested or used as collateral to fund your start-up. You can put money into your business as a loan or as equity. Talk to your accountant to determine which would be most beneficial for you. The danger is that you will not build into your plan enough of a return on that money to replace its lost earnings. And it will not be liquid while it is in your business, without shutting down the business. If you use all your savings, you will be without an emergency fund or retirement plan. Be careful.

Second, you can use personal money of family members. You could also use their borrowing ability without touching their money. Then, they become creditors or co-owners of your business. This arrangement is done all the time and creates some interesting family dynamics. If the investing family member is already in business, you will benefit from his or her experience at making a business go.

Third, nonfamily investors can be sought. This gets into more complicated securities laws, however. If you lose their money, you might be liable unless you follow a lot of very annoying rules. Your attorney can advise you on the appropriateness of this option in your situation. Most nonfamily investors will require a larger ownership share and a larger return on their investment, which will put more pressure on you as a new business owner.

Fourth, you can borrow the money from a lending institution. Most will require collateral, usually real estate or equipment. Second mortgages are a very common way to find business capital. Banks know how to do these loans and aren't as concerned about whether you have a solid business plan, even though they do want to see how you are going to repay the debt. They are very interested in the value of the collateral. Equipment can be leased from a variety of financial institutions if you have a good credit report. Even if you incorporate, you will be signing all these notes personally until your corporation develops its own credit after several years.

Fifth, you can investigate various government programs, which either grant or loan or guarantee loans to small businesses. Don't get your hopes up, though. They do happen, but to a very small percentage of those who apply.

Sixth, you can use trade credit. This is the most risky way to finance a business and usually can't be used for the entire capital needs. You may be able to locate suppliers who will stock your manufacturing line or your store with no cash for their merchandise. You will then need to pay them within 30/60/90 days.

Last, you may be able to find a supplier or a customer who is willing to finance you, either with a loan, an ownership share, or an advance payment for services. You will possibly limit your ability to do business with their competitors and this might be their motivation to get you going.

The three biggest mistakes new business owners make are as follows:

- Starting without knowing where the capital is coming from

- Forgetting to pay themselves

- Combining business and personal finance decisions

I'll discuss the second and third mistakes in the next section.

The biggest mistake that new business owners make is trying to get started without knowing where all their capital will come from. They get some seed money or spend their own savings until it is gone, believing that other investors will come through. They usually don't. What they end up doing is scaling down their business plan until there is no way to break even, and they fail. This is why you need to plan thoroughly before you start.

MY BEST ADVICE

Raising venture capital will be the hardest part of beginning your business. Don't begin an underfunded business, thinking that the money will come from somewhere.

How to Measure Success

The second biggest mistake that small business owners make is that they forget to pay themselves. This sounds a little silly, at first. Why else are they in business, except to make money? Well, you'd be surprised.

At first they are living off the invested money (theirs or some-one else's) and they feel as though they can't take their "full" salary. They'll kick it in when the business picks up. Then, they find they need more staff than they thought, so money is going to meet a payroll that they aren't on. Then, at some point, the work that they are doing is too much for them and they need to hire someone to do some of their tasks. This person is more expensive than the earlier employees. That puts even more stress on the cash flow. And so on.

This brings us back to my "working for myself" chuckle. As a start-up business, you probably can't afford you. If you have the talents to start a business, you are worth a lot on the job mar-ket. Eventually, you will expect to exceed that wage in your own company, or why would you take all the risk and endure all the headaches?

This brings us to a simple way to determine if you are running a successful company. Are you paying yourself what it would cost the business to replace your services to the company? And still making a profit? Even if you turn around and "reinvest" that paycheck in your company to enhance its growth and eventual value as an asset on your balance sheet, you still need to place a value on your own energies.

Many very new businesses have very sporadic cash flow. The owner will wait to take a paycheck when the big customer pays. The problem is that they don't take it over the next few paydays like their employees will. They take a chunk here and a chunk there. This muddies the question of whether they are paying themselves enough. So put yourself on the payroll at a salary that you would pay someone else to do your job. And wait for your paycheck like everyone else.

The third biggest mistake that small business owners make is that they commingle their business and personal financial decisions. The money may be very appropriately in separate accounts, with separate tax returns, but the decision-making is indistinguishable.

For example, they have a good sales week. The mortgage is due at home. The shop needs a new piece of equipment. Do they get the equipment or take a draw so they can pay their mortgage payment? These two issues should not even be discussed in the same conversation. If they are taking a paycheck as described above, and they don't have enough for the mortgage that week, it will be late. It has nothing to do with the equipment needs of the business, any more than any other employee's mortgage payment does.

The easiest measurement of success is when a business owner is operating both the business at a profit and the household with a balanced budget. And the decisions are kept separate.

MY BEST ADVICE

Put yourself on the payroll immediately, and keep your business and personal financial decisions separate.

What You Should Know by Now

1. What tax filings you will be responsible for if you become self-employed.

2. How much of your income will go to your tax and benefit costs as a self-employed individual.

3. How much you would need to bill as a consultant to equal your employed salary requirements.

4. What your business costs would be to be self-employed.

5. Where to go to learn how to write a business plan.

6. What the various sources available to you are to fund a small business.

7. How much you would pay yourself in such a business.

8. How to measure the success of a business you start.

Next Steps

1. _____
2. _____
3. _____
4. _____
5. _____
6. _____
7. _____
8. _____

Epilogue

Will You Be Ready If It Happens Again?

I should be asking you if you'll be ready *when* it happens again. Because it will. Just like car repairs, when we have something fixed, we drive away believing that the car will be fine for a long time. Last time I checked, fixing the brakes had no effect on the performance of the engine. But we still think we've bought some time.

How much time have you bought yourself in your new position? A year? Until the next recession? Well into retirement? Why is this one any different than the last? What stranger are you trusting this time?

You are excited and ready to go in your new position. I don't want to take that away from you, but I do want you to see where you are going this time. You are going to be there as long as it is working for you, and not a day longer than when it stops working for them.

You will put a total effort into your new responsibilities, your new relationships, and your new future. But realistically, how long is that future? When will you need to go do *something else* again? Will you be ready?

Readiness is a hard concept. It requires you to keep an eye on the downside, while staying motivated to work the upside. That's a conflict all by itself. But having a safety net lets you walk the high wire with confidence. You will need two safety nets: One for your mental well-being and one for your financial well-being. It's the attention to one that makes the other work.

Your safety net for your mental well-being is your life outside of work: your friends, your church, your community, your volunteer activities, and most of all, your family. If you build your life around work and it goes away, even temporarily, you suffer. Your safety net for your financial well-being is the foundation of your financial plan. Your insurance contracts outside of your employee benefits, your emergency savings strategies, your debt management strategies, and your retirement plan will all play an important part.

How you define your work will help you to keep a good perspective. Have you decided upon an identity that allows your job title to be a modifier? Are you seeing yourself as a free agent with skills that you can sell to anyone at anytime?

Remember that you *own* the real relationships in your life and those will always be there. But your relationship with your employer is *leased* for the specific time that it is productive. The most important relationship is the one you have with yourself. If you are confident of your skills and happy with your choices, you will be ready for the next change of scenery.

At the beginning of the book, I suggested that you capitalize on this temporary setback by developing strategies that would stay with you well beyond your recent period of unemployment. This would be the positive return from your layoff. You are a stronger person now, whether you feel it or not.

The financial decisions that you make from here on out will be different if you hold onto your recent experience. You will want to put it behind you and forget it. But not so fast! There are some great treasures hidden in what you're about to bury.

What was the greatest financial difficulty you had during your hiatus from employment? Be specific. Don't just say, "I didn't have enough money." Were your monthly payments too high? Did you rely on credit cards as your emergency fund? Did you have plenty of cushion, but cringed each time you needed to take some of it? Was too much of your savings tax deferred? Did your family fight too much about how to cut the budget? Were you relying on investments that weren't liquid or that lost their value during a slow economy? Did it take you longer than you thought it would to find employment, and your emergency funds ran out? Did you take a job you really didn't want because you had no other choice?

Being ready for the next job change means fixing the things that caused you the most stress. The hard part of this is that you have to start doing it now. You probably knew those things left you vulnerable, but you never got around to changing them. The only time that you have to fix them is right now. Other goals we've talked about, such as getting out of debt or resuming your retirement savings, can wait. The biggest threat to your security and all your other goals is not having a sufficient plan to weather a period of unemployment.

It's hard to plan for the unknown, but unemployment is known to you now. You know exactly what it looks like and what you don't like about it. Fix it. Don't put your money where it will be worthless or penalized at the exact time you need it. Don't think that your creditors will be pleasant when you don't have any income. Don't spend absolutely every penny you make, just to throw your family into financial meltdown when they have to cut the budget. Don't rely on your employer to purchase critical insurance products for you.

The world that you know is not normal, either geographically or historically. The type of employment "security" that the last two generations of Americans have experienced is new and certainly not universal. Many economies on the planet continue to experience their own *Grapes of Wrath* into our new century. Unemployment in many corners of the globe is regularly higher than our worst recession. Count your blessings, while counting on unemployment happening to you again. Next time, be ready.

Appendix

1.1: Greatest Fears

Think of as many words as you can to fill in the following blanks:

1. The first thing that flashed before my eyes when I knew I was losing my job was ...

   _____

   _____

2. The thing I just can't get out of my head is ...

   _____

   _____

3. The worst thing I've seen happen to someone who lost his or her job was ...

   _____

   _____

4. The thought that kept me awake last night was ...

   _____

   _____

5. I just know that _____ will happen.

6. I'd rather die than have _____ happen.

7. The person who is going to make me feel the worst about this is ...

_____

_____

1.2: Job Expectations

Fill in the blanks with as many answers as apply:

1. I applied for the job because ...

_____

_____

2. When I interviewed for the job they told me ...

_____

_____

3. I accepted the job because ...

_____

_____

4. I quickly learned that the job ...

_____

_____

5. I always expected the job to provide me with ...

_____

_____

6. The most important thing to my family was ...

_____

_____

7. The needs of mine that this job provided for were ...

_____

_____

1.3: What Worked Well with My Last Job

Think of as many examples as you can to fill in the following blanks:

1. Whenever _____
   happened, I felt good.

2. I would do the _____
   assignments before any other task.

3. The people I worked the best with had _____
   in common.

4. When I started this job, I never thought I would be
   able to ... _____
   _____

5. I was proud of my ability to _____
   in this job.

6. This job was better than any other job I've had because
   _____

7. My family liked _____
   the best about my job.

1.4: Positive Changes I Can Make for the Future

Think of as many examples as you can to fill in the following blanks:

1. I will be sure to _____
   as I meet my new co-workers.

2. I will work to improve my _____
   in my new job.

3. I will set goals in my new job that will enable me to ...

_____

_____

4. I will change the way I handle my ...

_____

_____

5. My money life will work better because I ...

_____

_____

6. As I make my benefit choices in my next job, I know I will change ...

_____

_____

7. I will respect myself the most as I accomplish ...

_____

_____

2.1: Proof of Unfairness

Finish the following statements as accurately as you can.

1. The people who must have known about this and didn't say anything to me were ...

    _____

    _____

2. When other companies have layoffs they don't ...

    _____

    _____

3. The way I was treated was ridiculous because ...

    _____

    _____

4. I can't believe they didn't pick _____ to be laid off before me.

5. If they knew they were laying me off, then why on Earth did they ...

    _____

    _____

6. I deserved more severance pay because ...

    _____

    _____

7. If they had just _____,
    they wouldn't have had to lay anybody off.

2.2: Job History

Go back to the beginning of your working life and fill in the
following table:

Employer	Whose Choice? Yours	Theirs	Whose Fault? Yours	Theirs
_____	___	___	___	___
_____	___	___	___	___
_____	___	___	___	___
_____	___	___	___	___
_____	___	___	___	___
_____	___	___	___	___
_____	___	___	___	___
_____	___	___	___	___
_____	___	___	___	___
_____	___	___	___	___
_____	___	___	___	___
_____	___	___	___	___
_____	___	___	___	___
Total number	___	___	___	___

2.3: Processing Anger

Try to be as honest as possible with your answers:

1. I am the angriest when I think about ...

   _____

   _____

2. What they did to me reminds me of ...

   _____

   _____

3. It would serve them right if ...

   _____

   _____

4. They don't know how much I could hurt them because ...

   _____

   _____

5. I have really thought about getting even by ...

   _____

   _____

6. A better way for me to deal with this is to ...

   _____

   _____

7. I can't afford to make any trouble because ...

   _____

   _____

2.4: Contacts to Keep

Name	Position	Department	Phone Number

3.1: Possible Feelings

Circle any words that describe something you've felt in the last few hours. Repeat the process daily until you are only choosing feelings that are normal for you:

Out of control	Peaceful	Fearful	Hopeful
Replaying the past	Living in the moment	Overwhelmed	Serene
Powerless	Letting go	Victimized	Responsible
Excited	Content	Anxious	Waiting
Angry	Expressive	Bored	Silent
Vulnerable	Secure	Punished	Patient
Discouraged	Faithful	Worthless	Wise
Shocked	Surprised	Looking	Learning
Lost	Reborn	Helpless	Finding opportunity
In hardship	Aspiring	Discouraged	Full of character
Obsessing over details	Celebrating	Living to work	Working to live
Unsuccessful	Undistracted	Disrespected	Dignified
Shut down	Starting over	Ruined	Rediscovered
Deprived	Satisfied	Imperfect	Performing
Unnecessary	Worthy	Numb	Sensitive

3.2: Possible Needs

Circle items on the list that you need right now. Look for respectful ways to communicate them to people who want to help you:

Compassion	Ideas	Space	Interaction
Respect	Stimulation	Love	Intimacy
Time Alone	Focus	Connections	Compassion
Sex	Financial advice	Food	Childcare
Wake-up call	Hair cut	Books	Church
Car to use	Reference letter	Support	Encouragement
Empathy	Time together	Listening	Friendship
Advice	Insight	Stories	Humor
A hug	Pat on the back	A loan	Clothes
Nothing	To be left alone	Excitement	Responsibility
Reassurance	Diversions	Normalcy	People to be happy
Help	Less responsibility	Peace	Prayers
A break	Closeness	Entertainment	New experiences

3.3: Common Signs of Depression

See how many of these symptoms are true for you. Check the appropriate column for each statement.

True	False	
_____	_____	My sleeping patterns are changing.
_____	_____	I am losing my appetite.
_____	_____	I'm not interested in anything.
_____	_____	I'm having trouble concentrating.
_____	_____	I'm losing interest in sex.
_____	_____	I am anxious and worried a lot.

Talk to your family doctor about these the next time you are in.

If you checked more than TWO TRUE STATEMENTS, make an appointment with a professional to talk about your symptoms now.

3.4: Family Communications

Fill in the name of each family member that you will want to tell. Pick a feeling from Appendix 3.1 and a need from Appendix 3.2 that you will share with them.

Family Member	Feeling	Need
_____	_____	_____
_____	_____	_____
_____	_____	_____
_____	_____	_____
_____	_____	_____
_____	_____	_____
_____	_____	_____
_____	_____	_____
_____	_____	_____
_____	_____	_____
_____	_____	_____

4.1: Questions for My Human Resources Department

Use the following space to record questions as you think of them. Check them off as you get your answers:

Question	Answer
_____	_____
_____	_____
_____	_____
_____	_____
_____	_____
_____	_____
_____	_____
_____	_____
_____	_____
_____	_____
_____	_____

4.2: Decisions That Can Wait

To clear your mind for more important immediate decisions, put those that can wait on this list and mark it with a date to work on it:

Decision	Due Date

5.1: Minimum Earnings or Employment Period Required to Qualify for Unemployment Benefits

State	Qualifying Wage or Employment
Alabama	$1^1/_2 \times$ high quarter wages
Alaska	$1,000; wages in two quarters
Arizona	$1^1/_2 \times$ high quarter wages; $1,000 in high quarter
Arkansas	27 × weekly benefit amount; wages in two quarters
California	$1,300 in high quarter or $900 in high quarter with base period wages = to $1^1/_4 \times$ high quarter
Colorado	40 × weekly benefit amount or $2,500 in base period, whichever is greater
Connecticut	40 × weekly benefit amount or $1^1/_2 \times$ high quarter wages
Delaware	36 × weekly benefit amount
Washington, D.C.	$1^1/_2 \times$ high quarter wages; not less than $1,950 in two quarters; $1,300 in one quarter
Florida	$1^1/_2 \times$ high quarter wages; $3,400 in base period
Georgia	150 percent of high quarter wages; wages in two quarters
Hawaii	26 × weekly benefit amount; wages in two quarters
Idaho	$1^1/_4 \times$ high quarter wage; not less than the minimum qualifying wages in one quarter; wages in two quarters
Illinois	$1,600; $440 outside high quarter
Indiana	Not less than $2,750; $1,650 in last two quarters

State	Qualifying Wage or Employment
Iowa	$1^1/_4 \times$ high quarter wage; 3.5 percent of the statewide average annual wage in high quarter; $^1/_2$ high quarter wage of second quarter
Kansas	30 × weekly benefit amount; wages in two quarters
Kentucky	$1^1/_2 \times$ high quarter wage; 8 × weekly benefit amount in last two quarters; $750 in one quarter, $750 in other quarters
Louisiana	$1,200; $1^1/_2 \times$ high quarter wage
Maine	2 × annual average weekly wage in each of two quarters, and 6 × annual average weekly wage in base period
Maryland	$1^1/_2 \times$ high quarter wage; $576.01 in one quarter; wages in two quarters
Massachusetts	30 × weekly benefit amount; not less than $2,700
Michigan	$1^1/_2 \times$ high quarter wage 20 weeks employment at 30 × state's minimum hourly wage
Minnesota	$1^1/_4 \times$ high quarter wage; at least $1,000 in high quarter; two quarters
Mississippi	40 × weekly benefit amount; $780 in one quarter; wages in two quarters
Missouri	$1^1/_2 \times$ high quarter wage; $1,000 in one quarter; wages in two quarters
Montana	$1^1/_2 \times$ high quarter wage; 7 percent of average annual wage in best period or 50 percent of average annual wage
Nebraska	$1,600; $800 in each of two quarters
Nevada	$1^1/_2 \times$ high quarter wage

State	Qualifying Wage or Employment
New Hampshire	$2,800; $1,400 in each of two quarters
New Jersey	20 weeks employment at 20 percent of average weekly wage; or 12 × average weekly wage
New Mexico	$1,324 in high quarter wage and wages in at least one other quarter
New York	$1^{1}/_{2}$ × high quarter wage; at least $1,600 in high quarter; wages in two quarters
North Carolina	At least $565.50 in best period; $1^{1}/_{2}$ = high quarter wage
North Dakota	$1^{1}/_{2}$ × high quarter wage
Ohio	20 weeks employment with wages in each week of 27.5 percent of state's average weekly wage
Oklahoma	$1,500; $1^{1}/_{2}$ × high quarter wage; $9,800
Oregon	$1^{1}/_{2}$ × high quarter wage; not less than $1,00 in best period or 500 hours of employment in the best period
Pennsylvania	$800 in high quarter; $1,320 in best period; at least 20 percent of best-period wages outside high quarter
Puerto Rico	40 × weekly benefit amount; not less than $280 best-period wages; $75 in one quarter; wages in two quarters
Rhode Island	Base period wages in two quarters of $1^{1}/_{2}$ × minimum taxable wage base for that year
South Carolina	$1^{1}/_{2}$ × high quarter wage; not less than $900; $540 in one quarter
South Dakota	$728 in high quarter; 20 × weekly benefit amount outside high quarter
Tennessee	40 × weekly benefit amount; $780.01 in highest two quarters
Texas	37 × weekly benefit amount; wages in at least two quarters

State	Qualifying Wage or Employment
Utah	$1^1/_2 \times$ high quarter wage
Vermont	$1,571 in a quarter; best period wages of 40 percent of total high quarter wages
Virginia	$2,500 to $13,400.01 in highest two quarters
Washington	680 hours
West Virginia	$2,200 and wages in two quarters
Wisconsin	30 × weekly benefit amount; 4 × weekly benefit amount outside high quarter
Wyoming	1.4 × high quarter wage; 8 percent of state's average annual wage in best period

5.2: State Unemployment Compensation Department Phone Numbers

Many states have local offices that will accept your claim over the phone. If your state is one of these, you will be referred to an office in your area by the operator at the number below.

State	Phone #
Alabama	866-234-5382
Alaska	1-888-252-2557
Arizona	602-364-2722
Arkansas	1-877-872-5627
California	1-800-300-5616
Colorado	303-318-8000
Connecticut	860-263-6000
Delaware	1-800-794-3032
Washington, D.C.	202-724-7000

State	Phone #
Florida	1-800-342-9909
Georgia	404-656-6000
Hawaii	808-586-8970
Idaho	208-334-4700
Illinois	1-888-337-7234
Indiana	1-888-967-5663
Iowa	800-562-4692
Kansas	1-800-292-6333
Kentucky	502-564-4761
Louisiana	225-342-3111
Maine	800-593-7660
Maryland	800-827-4839
Massachusetts	1-877-626-6800
Michigan	1-800-638-3995
Minnesota	1-877-898-9090
Mississippi	888-844-3577
Missouri	1-800-320-2519
Montana	1-800-207-0667
Nebraska	402-458-2500
Nevada	888-890-8211
New Hampshire	1-800-852-3400
New Jersey	888-795-6672
New Mexico	505-841-2000

State	Phone Number
New York	888-209-8124
North Carolina	877-841-9617
North Dakota	800-247-0981
Ohio	1-877-644-6562
Oklahoma	1-800-555-1554
Oregon	1-800-982-8920
Pennsylvania	1-888-313-7284
Rhode Island	401-462-8000
South Carolina	866-831-1724
South Dakota	605-626-2452
Tennessee	1-877-813-0950
Texas	1-800-939-6631
Utah	1-888-848-0688
Vermont	1-877-214-3330
Virginia	800-552-7945
Washington	800-318-6022
West Virginia	304-558-2657
Wisconsin	1-800-822-5246
Wyoming	307-473-3789

5.3: State Websites for Information on Unemployment Insurance

State	Website
Alabama	https://dir.alabama.gov/uc/claims
Alaska	www.labor.state.ak.us/esd_unemployment_insurance/home.htm
Arizona	www.de.state.az.us/links/esa/index.html
Arkansas	www.state.ar.us/esd/WorkersUnempBenefits/ADWS_Workerunempben.htm
California	www.state.ca.us/Employment/UnemployDis.html
Colorado	www.colorado.gov/cs/Satellite/CO-Portal/CXP/1174084100247
Connecticut	www.ctdol.state.ct.us/progsupt/unemplt/unemployment.htm
Delaware	https://joblink.delaware.gov/ada
Washington, D.C.	http://does.dc.gov/does/cwp/view%2Ca%2C1232%2Cq%2C640720.asp
Florida	https://www2.myflorida.com/fluid
Georgia	www.dol.state.ga.us/js/unemployment_benefits_individuals.htm
Hawaii	www.dlir.state.hi.us/uitext.html
Idaho	http://labor.idaho.gov/dnn/idl/UnemploymentInsurance/UIBenefits/tabid/681/Default.aspx
Illinois	www.ides.state.il.us
Indiana	www.state.in.us/dwd/2345.htm
Iowa	www.iowaworkforce.org/ui
Kansas	www.dol.ks.gov/ui/html/faqs_BUS.html

State	Website
Kentucky	www.desky.org
Louisiana	www.laworks.net/uifaq.asp
Maine	www.state.me.us/labor/uibennys/index.htm
Maryland	www.dllr.state.md.us/employment/unemployment.shtml
Massachusetts	www.detma.org/claimant/
Michigan	www.michiganworks.org
Minnesota	www.uimn.org
Mississippi	www.ms.gov/ms_sub_sub_template.jsp?Category_ID=7010
Missouri	www.dolir.mo.gov/es
Montana	http://uid.dli.mt.gov
Nebraska	www.dol.state.ne.us/nwd/center.cfm?PRICAT=1&SUBCAT=1B
Nevada	http://detr.state.nv.us/uiben/uiben_uiben.htm
New Hampshire	https://claims.nhes.state.nh.us/weblogic/Home.jsp
New Jersey	http://lwd.dol.state.nj.us/labor/ui/ui_index.html
New Mexico	www.dol.state.nm.us/dol_quib.html
New York	www.labor.state.ny.us/ui/ui_index.shtm
North Carolina	www.ncesc.com/splash.asp
North Dakota	www.jobsnd.com
Ohio	http://unemployment.ohio.gov
Oklahoma	www.oesc.state.ok.us/UI/default.shtm
Oregon	www.oregon.gov/EMPLOY/UI/index.shtml
Pennsylvania	www.dli.state.pa.us/landi/taxonomy/taxonomy.asp?DLN=853

State	Website
Puerto Rico	www.gobierno.pr/ADT/Servicios/Desempleo.htm
Rhode Island	www.dlt.state.ri.us/ui
South Carolina	www.sces.org/ui/Index.htm
South Dakota	http://dol.sd.gov
Tennessee	www.state.tn.us/labor-wfd/esdiv.html
Texas	www.twc.state.tx.us/ui/uiclaim.html
Utah	http://jobs.utah.gov/ui
Vermont	www.labor.vermont.gov
Virgin Islands	www.vidol.gov/Units/Unemployment_Insurance/UI.htm
Virginia	www.vec.virginia.gov/vecportal/unins/insunemp.cfm
Washington	www.esd.wa.gov/uibenefits/index.php
West Virginia	www.wvbep.org/bep/uc
Wisconsin	www.dwd.state.wi.us/ui
Wyoming	http://wydoe.state.wy.us/doe.asp?ID=11

5.4: Weekly Benefit Calculation

State	Weekly Benefit Calculation	Minimum	Maximum
Alabama	$1/24$ of average of two highest quarters	$45	$190
Alaska	4.4 – 0.9 percent of annual wages + $24 per dependent up to $72	$44–$116	$248–$320
Arizona	$1/25$ of highest quarter wages	$40	$205
Arkansas	$1/26$ of highest quarter wages up to $66^2/_3$ percent of state's average weekly wage	$57	$321

State	Weekly Benefit Calculation	Minimum	Maximum
California	$1/_{23} - 1/_{33}$ of highest quarter wages (if high quarter wages exceed $4,066.00, the max weekly benefit amount will be 39 percent of these wages divided by 13)	$40	$230
Colorado	60 percent of $1/_{26}$ of claimant's two highest quarters up to 50 percent of $1/_{52}$ of average weekly wage	$25	$358
Connecticut	$1/_{26}$ of average of two highest quarters up to 60 percent of state's average weekly wage + $15 per dependent up to five dependents, no more than weekly benefit amount	$15–30	$397–472
Delaware	$1/_{46}$ of wages in highest two quarters, if the trust fund balance is at least $90 million, or as $1/_{52}$ of wages in highest two quarters, if the trust fund balance is less than $90 million	$20	$315
Washington, D.C.	$1/_{26}$ of highest quarter wages, up to 50 percent of state's average weekly wage	$50	$309
Florida	$1/_{26}$ of highest quarter wages	$32	$275
Georgia	$1/_{48}$ of two highest quarters wages	$39	$274
Hawaii	$1/_{20}$ of highest quarter wages up to 70 percent of state's average weekly wage	$5	$371
Idaho	$1/_{26}$ of highest quarter wages up to 60 percent of state's average weekly wage	$51	$296
Illinois	49.5 percent of claimant's average weekly wage in two highest quarters up to 49.5 percent of state's average weekly wage	$51–56	$296–392

State	Weekly Benefit Calculation	Minimum	Maximum
Indiana	5 percent of first $2,000 in high quarter, 4 percent of remaining high quarter wages	$50	$288
Iowa	$1/_{19} - 1/_{23}$ of highest quarter wages up to 65 percent of state's average weekly wage for claimants with dependents	$40–49	$273–335
Kansas	4.25 percent of high quarter wage up to 60 percent of state's average weekly wage	$80	$320
Kentucky	1.3078 percent of best period wages up to 62 percent of state's average weekly wage	$39	$329
Louisiana	$1/_{25}$ of 4 quarters average wages	$10	$258
Maine	$1/_{22}$ of highest quarter wages up to 52 percent of state's average weekly wage + $10 per dependent up to weekly benefit amount	$46–$69	$265–$397
Maryland	$1/_{24}$ of high quarter wage + $8 per dependent up to 4	$25–$57	$280
Massachusetts	50 percent of average weekly wage up to 57.5 percent of state's average weekly wage, + $25 per dependent up to $1/_2$ weekly benefit amount	$29–$43	$477–$715
Michigan	4.1 percent of high quarter wage plus $6 for each dependent, up to 5	$88–$118	$300
Minnesota	Higher of 50 percent of the individual's average weekly wage during the base period, to a maximum of $66^2/_3$ percent of the state's average weekly wage; or 50 percent of the individual's average weekly wage during the high quarter to a maximum of 50 percent of the state's average weekly wage, or $331, whichever is higher	$38	$331–$427

State	Weekly Benefit Calculation	Minimum	Maximum
Mississippi	$1/26$ of high quarter wage	$30	$190
Missouri	4.0 percent of high quarter wage	$40	$235
Montana	1 percent of best period wages or 1.0 percent of wages in two high quarters up to 60 percent of state's average weekly wage	$65	$263
Nebraska	$1/2$ average weekly wage	$36	$252
Nevada	$1/25$ of highest quarter wages, up to 50 percent of state's average weekly wage	$16	$291
New Hampshire	1.0 – 1.1 percent of annual wages	$32	$301
New Jersey	60 percent of claimant's average weekly wage + dependent allowances up to $56^2/_3$ percent of state's average weekly wage	$61–$70	$429
New Mexico	$1/26$ of high quarter wage; not less than 10 percent nor more than 50 percent of state's average weekly wage	$50	$267
New York	$1/26$ of high quarter wage unless less than $3,575 then $1/25$	$40	$405
North Carolina	$1/26$ of high quarter up to $66^2/_3$ percent of state's average weekly wage	$30	$375
North Dakota	$1/65$ of the two highest quarters; and $1/2$ total wages in the third quarter, up to 62 percent of the state's average weekly wage	$43	$293
Ohio	$1/2$ claimant's average weekly wage + dependent allowance of $1 to $83 based on claimant's average weekly wage and number of dependents	$77	$289–$389

State	Weekly Benefit Calculation	Minimum	Maximum
Oklahoma	$1/23$ of high quarter wage	$16	$291
Oregon	$1/25$ of base-period wages up to 64 percent of state's average weekly wage	$88	$376
Pennsylvania	$1/23 - 1/25$ of highest quarter wages up to $66 2/3$ percent of state's average weekly wage + $5 for one dependent; + $3 for second	$35-$43	$430-$438
Puerto Rico	$1/11 - 1/26$ of highest quarter wages; up to 50 percent of state's average weekly wage	$7	$133
Rhode Island	4.62 percent of high quarter wage up to 67 percent of state's average weekly wage + greater of $10, or + 5 percent of the benefit rate per dependent up to 5 dependents	$56-$106	$397-$496
South Carolina	$1/26$ of highest quarter wages up to $65 2/3$ percent of state's average weekly wage	$20	$259
South Dakota	$1/26$ of highest quarter wages up to 50 percent of state's average weekly wage	$28	$224
Tennessee	$1/26$ of average two highest quarters	$30	$255
Texas	$1/25$ of high quarter wage	$49	$294
Utah	$1/26$ of highest quarter wages up to 60 percent of state's insured average fiscal year weekly wage	$22	$355
Vermont	Wages in the two highest quarters divided by 45	$298	$331

State	Weekly Benefit Calculation	Minimum	Maximum
Virginia	$1/_{50}$ of the two highest quarters	$50	$268
Washington	$1/_{25}$ of average two highest quarters wages up to 70 percent of state's average weekly wage	$94	$441
West Virginia	1.0 percent of annual wages up to $66^2/_3$ percent of state's average weekly wage	$24	$327
Wisconsin	4 percent of high quarter wage up to maximum weekly benefit amount	$46	$313
Wyoming	4 percent of high quarter wage up to 55 percent of state's average weekly wage	$20	$281

5.5: Earnings Disregarded: The Amount You May Earn Before Your Unemployment Benefit Is Reduced

State	Earnings Disregarded
Alabama	$15
Alaska	$1/_4$ wages over $50
Arizona	$30
Arkansas	$2/_5$ of wages
California	Greater of $25 or 25 percent of base period wages
Colorado	$1/_4$ weekly benefit amount
Connecticut	$1/_3$ of wages
Delaware	Greater of $10 or 30 percent of weekly benefit amount
Washington, D.C.	$1/_5$ of wages
Florida	8 × federal hourly minimum wage
Georgia	$30

State	Earnings Disregarded
Hawaii	$50
Idaho	$1/2$ weekly benefit amount
Illinois	$1/2$ weekly benefit amount
Indiana	Greater of $3 or 20 percent of weekly benefit amount from other than base period employer
Iowa	25 percent of weekly benefit amount
Kansas	25 percent of weekly benefit amount
Kentucky	$1/5$ of wages
Louisiana	Lesser of $1/2$ weekly benefit amount or $50
Maine	$25
Maryland	$70
Massachusetts	$1/3$ weekly benefit amount
Michigan	For each $1 earned the weekly benefit amount will be reduced by 50¢; there is also a limitation on total weekly benefits and earnings at $1 1/2$ times the benefit amount with an equal reduction of benefits for each $1 earned
Minnesota	Greater of $50 or 25 percent of wages
Mississippi	$40
Missouri	$20
Montana	$1/2$ wages in excess of $1/4$ weekly best average
Nebraska	$1/2$ weekly best average
Nevada	$1/4$ wages
New Hampshire	30 percent of weekly best average
New Jersey	Greater of $5 or $1/5$ weekly best average
New Mexico	$1/5$ weekly best average

State	Earnings Disregarded
New York	Waiting period is four effective days accumulated in one to four weeks; partial benefits $1/4$ weekly benefit amount for each one to three effective days. Effective days: fourth and each subsequent day of total unemployment in week for which not more than $300 is paid.
North Carolina	10 percent average weekly wage in high quarter
North Dakota	60 percent of weekly best average
Ohio	$1/5$ weekly best average
Oklahoma	$100
Oregon	$1/3$ weekly best average or 10 × the state's minimum wage
Pennsylvania	Greater of $6 or 40 percent weekly benefit amount
Puerto Rico	Weekly benefit amount
Rhode Island	$1/5$ weekly benefit amount
South Carolina	$1/4$ weekly benefit amount
South Dakota	$1/4$ wages over $25
Tennessee	Greater of $50 or 25 percent of weekly benefit amount
Texas	Greater of $5 or $1/4$ weekly benefit amount
Utah	30 percent of weekly benefit amount
Vermont	Greater of 30 percent of weekly benefit amount or $40
Virginia	$25
Washington	25 percent in excess of $15
West Virginia	$60
Wisconsin	$30 plus 33 percent of wages in excess of $30
Wyoming	50 percent of weekly benefit amount

6.1: Your Transitional Budget

Estimate the cost of each item for your average monthly expenditure and then think about whether it could be reduced temporarily.

Current Amount	Could Reduce To	Budget Item
CASH		
Groceries	_____	_____
Entertainment	_____	_____
Gasoline	_____	_____
Day care	_____	_____
_____	_____	_____
_____	_____	_____
BILLS		
Mortgage/rent	_____	_____
Electric	_____	_____
Heat	_____	_____
Water/trash	_____	_____
Phone	_____	_____
Cable/Internet	_____	_____

Current Amount	Could Reduce To	Budget Item
BILLS		
Car insurance	_____	_____
Life insurance	_____	_____
Health insurance	_____	_____
_____	_____	_____
_____	_____	_____

DEBTS

Car loan _____ _____

Credit card _____ _____

_____ _____ _____

_____ _____ _____

PERIODIC EXPENSES

Medical _____ _____

Clothing _____ _____

Car repairs _____ _____

_____ _____ _____

_____ _____ _____

_____ _____ _____

6.2: Sources of Income

Think of as many different ways to generate extra income in the following categories and estimate how much you could bring in over the next three months.

Unemployment Insurance Benefits $_____

Part-time employment outside field

_____ $_____

_____ $_____

_____ $_____

Part-time/consulting in career field

_____ $_____

_____ $_____

_____ $_____

Other family members that can increase income

_____ $_____

_____ $_____

_____ $_____

Jobs that will reduce my expenses

_____ $_____

_____ $_____

_____ $_____

Income-generating investments

_____ $_____

_____ $_____

_____ $_____

Assets that can be sold

_____ $_____

_____ $_____

_____ $_____

Assets that can be leased/rented

_____ $_____

_____ $_____

_____ $_____

Final payments from employer that can be used to supplement income

_____ $_____

_____ $_____

_____ $_____

Total all the sources: $_____

÷ 3

Monthly Income $_____

6.3: Transitional Expenses

Fill in the chart to begin to plan how much you will need to make this transition and how you will fund this need.

Expense	Estimated Amount	Source of Funds
Resumé/computer expenses		
_____	$_____	_____
_____	$_____	_____
Interviewing expenses		
_____	$_____	_____
_____	$_____	_____
Personal care expenses		
_____	$_____	_____
_____	$_____	_____
Professional services		
_____	$_____	_____
_____	$_____	_____
Networking expenses		
_____	$_____	_____
_____	$_____	_____

6.4: Sample Agenda for a Weekly Family Meeting

Spend some time at your first family meeting reviewing this agenda and adjusting it for your needs:

I. Agree to the ending time for this meeting and the starting time for the next meeting.

II. Agree to the ground rules of ...

    A. Respect.

    B. Confidentiality.

    C. Positive tones.

III. Review the accomplishments and disappointment of the previous week allowing everyone a turn to talk.

IV. Financial reports

    A. Bank account balances

    B. Income received during the week

    C. Expenses/bills paid out during the week

    D. Income expected for the coming week

    E. Expenses/bills expected for the coming week

    F. Problems or challenges expected

V. Project the activities and goals for the coming week allowing everyone a turn to talk.

VI. Assign each family member at least one task that relates to the activities and goals for the week.

7.1: State Department of Insurance Websites and Phone Numbers

State	Website	Phone Number
Alabama	www.aldoi.org	334-269-3550
Alaska	www.dced.state.ak.us/insurance/	907-465-2515
Arizona	www.id.state.az.us	1-800-544-9208
Arkansas	www.state.ar.us/insurance/	1-800-282-9134
California	www.insurance.ca.gov	1-800-927-4357
Colorado	www.dora.state.co.us/insurance/	1-800-930-3745
Connecticut	www.ct.gov/cid/site/default.asp	1-800-203-3447
Delaware	www.state.de.us/inscom/	302-739-4251
Washington D.C.	www.disb.dc.gov	202-727-8000
Florida	www.fldfs.com	850-413-3100
Georgia	www.inscomm.state.ga.us	1-800-656-2298
Hawaii	www.state.hi.us/dcca/ins/	808-586-2790
Idaho	www.doi.idaho.gov	1-800-721-3272
Illinois	www.state.il.us/ins/default.htm	217-782-4515
Indiana	www.in.gov/idoi	317-232-2385
Iowa	www.iid.state.ia.us/	1-877-955-1212

State	Website	Phone Number
Kansas	www.ksinsurance.org	1-800-432-2484
Kentucky	www.doi.state.ky.us/	1-800-595-6053
Louisiana	www.ldi.la.gov/	1-800-259-5300
Maine	www.state.me.us/pfr/ins/ins/index/htm	1-800-300-5000
Maryland	www.mdinsurance.state.md.us	1-800-492-6116
Massachusetts	www.state.ma.us/doi	1-888-283-3757
Michigan	www.cis.state.mi.us/ofis/	517-373-1820
Minnesota	www.commerce.state.mn.us/	1-800-657-3602
Mississippi	www.mid.state.ms.us	1-800-562-2957
Missouri	www.insurance.mo.gov	1-800-726-7390
Montana	www.discoveringmontana.com/sao	406-444-2040
Nebraska	www.doi.ne.gov	1-877-564-7323
Nevada	www.doi.state.nv.us/	775-687-4270
New Hampshire	www.state.nh.us/insurance	1-800-852-3416
New Jersey	www.state.nj.us/dobi/index.html	1-800-446-7467
New Mexico	www.nmprc.state.nm.us/inshm.htm	1-888-427-5772
New York	www.ins.state.ny.us	1-800-342-3736
North Carolina	www.ncdoi.com	1-800-546-5664
North Dakota	www.state.nd.us/ndins	1-800-247-0560
Ohio	www.ohioinsurance.gov/	614-644-2658
Oklahoma	www.oid.state.ok.us	1-800-522-0071
Oregon	www.cbs.state.or.us/external/ins	1-888-877-4894
Pennsylvania	www.insurance.state.pa.us/	1-877-881-6388

State	Website	Phone Number
Puerto Rico	www.ocs.gobierno.pr/	787-722-8686
Rhode Island	www.dbr.state.ri.us	401-462-9500
South Carolina	www.doi.sc.gov	803-737-6180
South Dakota	www.state.sd.us/drr2/reg	605-773-3563
Tennessee	www.state.tn.us/commerce/	615-741-4737
Texas	www.tdi.state.tx.us	1-800-252-3439
Utah	www.insurance.state.ut.us	801-538-3800
Vermont	www.bishca.state.vt.us/ InsurDiv/insur_index.htm	1-800-964-1784
Virginia	www.state.va.us/scc/division/ boi/index.htm	1-800-552-7945
Washington	www.insurance.wa.gov	1-800-562-6900
West Virginia	www.state.wv.us/insurance	1-888-879-9842
Wisconsin	http://oci.wi.gov	1-800-236-8517
Wyoming	insurance.state.wy.us/	1-800-438-5768

7.2: State Offices of Workers' Compensation Websites and Phone Numbers

State	Website	Phone Number
Alabama	http://dir.alabama.gov/wc	1-866-234-5382
Alaska	www.labor.state.ak.us/wc/wc.htm	907-465-2790
Arizona	www.statefund.com	602-631-2300
Arkansas	www.awcc.state.ar.us/	1-800-622-4472
California	www.scif.com	415-565-1472
Colorado	workerscomp.cdle.state.co.us/	1-888-390-7936

State	Website	Phone Number
Connecticut	wcc.state.ct.us/	860-493-1500
Delaware	www.delawareworks.com/ industrialaffairs/services/ workerscomp.shtml	302-761-8200
Washington D.C.	www.workerscompensation.com/ washington_dc.php	202-576-6265
Florida	www.fldfs.com/wc	850-413-1601
Georgia	http://sbwc.georgia.gov/02/ sbwc/home/ 0,2235,11394008,00.html	1-800-436-7442
Hawaii	www.hemic.com	808-524-3642
Idaho	www.state.id.us/isif/index.htm	1-800-334-2370
Illinois	www.state.il.us/agency/iic/	312-814-6611
Indiana	www.in.gov/wkcomp/index.html	1-800-457-8283
Iowa	www.state.ia.us/iwd/wc/index.html	1-800-562-4692
Kansas	www.hr.state.ks.us/wc.html/ wc.htm	1-800-292-6333
Kentucky	http://labor.ky.gov/ workersclaims	502-564-5550
Louisiana	www.ldol.state.la.us/ sec2owca.asp	1-800-259-5154
Maine	www.state.me.us/wcb	207-287-3751
Maryland	www.wcc.state.md.us	1-800-492-0479
Massachusetts	www.state.ma.us/dia/	1-800-323-3249
Michigan	www.michigan.gov/uia	517-322-1296
Minnesota	www.doli.state.mn.us/workcomp.html	1-800-342-5354
Mississippi	www.mwcc.state.ms.us	1-866-473-6922

State	Website	Phone Number
Missouri	www.dolir.mo.gov	573-751-4091
Montana	stfund.state.mt.us/	406-444-6500
Nebraska	www.nol.org/home/WC/	1-800-599-5155
Nevada	www.workerscompensation.com/nevada.php	775-684-7555
New Hampshire	www.labor.state.nh.us	603-271-3176
New Jersey	http://lwd.dol.state.nj.us/labor/wc/wc_index.html	609-292-2414
New Mexico	www.workerscomp.state.nm.us	1-800-255-7965
New York	www.nysif.com	1-888-875-5790
North Carolina	www.ic.nc.gov	919-807-2500
North Dakota	www.workforcesafety.com	1-800-777-5033
Ohio	www.ohiobwc.com	1-800-644-6292
Oklahoma	www.okcomp.com	405-232-7663
Oregon	www.saif.com	1-800-285-8525
Pennsylvania	www.workerscompensationinsurance.com/workers_compensation/pennsylvania.htm	1-800-482-2383
Puerto Rico	www.cfsepr.com	787-781-5040
Rhode Island	www.beaconmutual.com	401-825-2667
South Carolina	www.wcc.state.sc.us	803-737-5700
South Dakota	http://dol.sd.gov/workerscomp/default.aspx	605-773-3681
Tennessee	www.state.tn.us/labor-wfd/wcomp.html	615-741-6642

State	Website	Phone Number
Texas	www.txfund.com	1-800-859-5995
Utah	www.laborcommission.utah.gov/IndustrialAccidents/index.html	801-530-6800
Vermont	www.state.vt.us/labind/wcindex.htm	802-828-2286
Virginia	www.vwc.state.va.us	804-367-8600
Washington	www.wa.gov/lni/insurance/	360-902-4200
West Virginia	www.wvwcc.org/handcrafted2.asp	1-800-628-4265
Wisconsin	www.dwd.state.wi.us/wc/default.htm	608-266-1340
Wyoming	www.wydoe.state.wy.us	307-777-7159

9.1: Credit Reporting Agencies

To request a free credit report because you are unemployed, you will need to gather the following information and *mail* in your request:

- Full legal name
- Current mailing address (two forms of proof are needed for mail requests)
- Previous mailing addresses for last five years
- Date of birth
- Social Security number
- Telephone number
- Signature
- Signed statement that you are unemployed and seeking employment within 60 days

Experian

Experian
PO Box 2002
Allen, TX 75013
1-888-EXPERIAN (1-888-397-3742)
Hearing impaired 1-800-972-0322
www.experian.com

TransUnion

TransUnion LLC
Consumer Disclosure Center
PO Box 1000
Chester, PA 19022
1-800-888-4213
www.transunion.com

Equifax

Equifax Inc.
PO Box 740241
Atlanta, GA 30374
1-800-685-1111
www.equifax.com

9.2: Existing Indebtedness

Fill in the chart completely. Call your creditors if you can't find the information.

Creditor	Balance	Limit	Minimum	Due Date	Late Fee
_____	_____	_____	_____	_____	_____
_____	_____	_____	_____	_____	_____
_____	_____	_____	_____	_____	_____
_____	_____	_____	_____	_____	_____
_____	_____	_____	_____	_____	_____
_____	_____	_____	_____	_____	_____
_____	_____	_____	_____	_____	_____

10.1: The True Cost of Owning Your Home

Fill in all *yearly* figures for each column:

	Own	Rent
Cash Flow Items		
1. Annual Mortgage Payment or Rent	+ _____	+ _____
2. Plus: Condominium Fees	+ _____	
3. Plus: Real-Estate Taxes	+ _____	
4. Plus: Maintenance (3% of property value)	+ _____	+ _____
5. Plus: Electric/Heat/Water/Trash	+ _____	+ _____
6. Less: Income earned on Equity Cashed out of Home (at 4%)	− _____	
ANNUAL CASH FLOW COST	= _____	= _____
Tax and Appreciation Items		
7. Less: Principal Repaid on Loan	− _____	
8. Plus: Tax on Income earned in 6.		+ _____
9. Less: Tax Savings due to Deductibility of Interest and Property Taxes	− _____	
10. Less: Appreciation on House (2%)	− _____	
ANNUAL NET COST	= _____	= _____

11.1: Your Balance Sheet Assets

List each asset you own, and estimate the different values that it has:

Asset	Purchase Price	Cash Value	Depreciated Value	Replacement Value	Income Producing
Cash Assets					
___	___	___	___	___	___
___	___	___	___	___	___
___	___	___	___	___	___
Use Assets					
___	___	___	___	___	___
___	___	___	___	___	___
___	___	___	___	___	___
___	___	___	___	___	___
___	___	___	___	___	___
___	___	___	___	___	___
Investment Assets					
___	___	___	___	___	___
___	___	___	___	___	___
Investment Assets					
___	___	___	___	___	___
___	___	___	___	___	___
___	___	___	___	___	___
___	___	___	___	___	___

11.2: Emotional Value of Your Assets

List all the assets you own, and assign them an emotional value in your life:

Asset	Strongly Like	Like	Neutral	Dislike	Strongly Dislike
_____	____	____	____	____	____
_____	____	____	____	____	____
_____	____	____	____	____	____
_____	____	____	____	____	____
_____	____	____	____	____	____
_____	____	____	____	____	____
_____	____	____	____	____	____
_____	____	____	____	____	____
_____	____	____	____	____	____
_____	____	____	____	____	____
_____	____	____	____	____	____
_____	____	____	____	____	____
_____	____	____	____	____	____
_____	____	____	____	____	____
_____	____	____	____	____	____

11.3: How Long Will Your Money Last?

Fill in the following monthly numbers to see when you need to begin to sell other assets:

Income

Severance Pay   _____

Unemployment Benefits   _____

Supplemental Income   _____

    Total Income   _____

Expenses

Cash   _____

Bills   _____

Debts   _____

Periodic Expenses   _____

Transitional Expenses   _____

    Total Expenses   _____

    Shortfall (Income – Expenses)   _____

   Cash Assets ÷ Shortfall = _____ Months

12.1: Body, Mind, and Spirit

Think of simple ways to keep yourself growing healthier in these three areas:

Activity	Frequency	Cost
Body		
_____	_____	_____
_____	_____	_____
_____	_____	_____
_____	_____	_____
Mind		
_____	_____	_____
_____	_____	_____
_____	_____	_____
_____	_____	_____
Spirit		
_____	_____	_____
_____	_____	_____
_____	_____	_____
_____	_____	_____

12.2: Your Best Culture

Fill in the following blanks with as many words as you can think of to discover what you think is "normal" in a business environment:

1. I was shocked when my friend told me that they _____ at their company.

_____

_____

2. I always wished that my company would have _____ more often.

_____

_____

3. The hardest thing to get used to when I started my last job was ... _____

_____

_____

4. There were arguments all the time about _____ at my last company.

_____

_____

5. Everyone in the department would have the best time at _____.

_____

_____

6. I really thought _____ would never fit in there because _____.

_____

_____

7. I've always wanted to work in a place where they ...

_____

_____

_____

12.3: Fun and Cheap

Think of the most fun you can have for the least amount of money, and fill in the blanks. Next time you are bored, check the list.

Projects I Haven't Finished

_____   _____

_____   _____

_____   _____

_____   _____

Hobbies That Relax Me

_____   _____

_____   _____

_____   _____

_____   _____

Places I Could Visit

_____   _____

_____   _____

_____   _____

_____   _____

13.1: Work Schedule

Be your own boss and give yourself a work schedule and daily goals to balance the following assignments:

- Research
- Networking
- Searching Job Postings
- Sending Out Resumés
- Scheduling Interviews
- Interviewing
- Follow-Up Calls

Time	Task	Daily Goal	Accomplished
8:00 A.M.			
9:00 A.M.			
10:00 A.M.			
11:00 A.M.			
12:00 P.M.			
1:00 P.M.			
2:00 P.M.			
3:00 P.M.			
4:00 P.M.			
5:00 P.M.			
6:00 P.M.			
7:00 P.M.			
8:00 P.M.			

13.2: Job Criteria

Fill in the blanks for the following criteria. Then rank each criterion as to its importance in your search.

Criteria	Specifics Important to You	Rank
Work Schedule	_____	____
Schedule Flexibility	_____	____
Location	_____	____
Transportation to Work	_____	____
Industry	_____	____
Salary	_____	____
Benefits Package	_____	____
Job Title	_____	____
Job Duties	_____	____
Size of Company	_____	____
Age of Company	_____	____
Profitability of Company	_____	____
Dress Code	_____	____
Company Culture	_____	____
Other	_____	____
Other	_____	____

14.1: Comparing Offers

Reducing each aspect of your job offer to a dollar equivalent can help you see how it stacks up against your last job and other offers. You may use monthly or yearly numbers, whichever is easier for you.

Income Item	Last Job	Offer #1	Offer #2	Offer #3
Wages/Salary				
Sick/Vacation Pay				
Commission/Bonus				
Pension Contribution				
Benefits Contribution				
Other				
Gross Income				
Work Expenses				
Mileage @ $.34				
Public Trans.				
Work Clothing				
Workplace Culture				
Workplace Charities				
Day Care Expense				
Personal Care				
Total Expenses				
Net Income				

14.2: Work Conditions

As you receive job offers, fill in the following chart to remind yourself of the importance of your top-10 list:

TOP FIVE THINGS THAT SHOULD BE THE SAME AS MY LAST JOB

	Offer #1	Offer #2	Offer #3
1. _____	_____	_____	_____
2. _____	_____	_____	_____
3. _____	_____	_____	_____
4. _____	_____	_____	_____
5. _____	_____	_____	_____

TOP FIVE THINGS THAT SHOULD BE DIFFERENT FROM MY LAST JOB

	Offer #1	Offer #2	Offer #3
1. _____	_____	_____	_____
2. _____	_____	_____	_____
3. _____	_____	_____	_____
4. _____	_____	_____	_____
5. _____	_____	_____	_____

Index

D

E–F

About the Author

Edie Milligan Driskill has worked for 20 years to help shape the emerging field of financial counseling through her work with social-service agencies and families from all income levels. She has designed and delivered financial programs that combine the best practices from the fields of Social Work and Financial Planning. She has achieved the credentials of Certified Financial Planner, Chartered Life Underwriter, and Accredited Financial Counselor. She serves on the Board of the Association for Financial Counseling and Planning Education, and has been active in the National Council on Problem Gambling and the Employee Assistance Professionals Association. She is the author of *Take Charge: A Woman's Guide to a Secure Retirement*.